ABOUT THE AUTHOR

David Chilton is the president of a consulting firm that specializes in teaching financial planning techniques through employer-sponsored seminars. By combining common sense and humour, Dave has shown hundreds of thousands of people that sound financial planning is, indeed, "pretty simple stuff." A frequent guest on national TV and radio shows, and a much sought-after speaker, Dave lives in Kitchener, Ontario, with his wife, Susan, son, Scott, daughter, Courtney, and their wonder-dog, Charley.

The
Wealthy
Barber

The Wealthy Barber

THE COMMON SENSE GUIDE TO SUCCESSFUL FINANCIAL PLANNING

DAVID CHILTON

Stoddart

Published in 1989 by
Stoddart Publishing Co. Limited
34 Lesmill Road
Toronto, Canada
M3B 2T6

Thirty-sixth printing
February 1994

Chilton, David Barr, 1961-
The wealthy barber

ISBN 0-7737-5318-4

1. Finance, Personal.   I. Title.

HG179.C45 1989   332.024'01   C89-094533-0

Editor: Susan Daminato
Cover Design: Brant Cowie/ArtPlus Limited
Typesetting: Tony Gordon Ltd.
Printed in Canada

To Susan

CONTENTS

PREFACE

The wisest tips on how to develop a financial plan are of little use if they are not conveyed in an understandable manner — a manner that responds effectively to the questions and concerns of the reader. Likewise, the most articulately expressed thoughts on finance may be wasted if they are not presented in an entertaining style — a style that maintains the interest of the reader.

So how does one write an understandable and entertaining financial planning book?

I hope and believe that *The Wealthy Barber* answers that question, by taking a "novel" approach to the teaching of financial planning.

Rather than inundating you with intimidating charts and graphs and a series of lifeless numbers, *The Wealthy Barber* will both entertain and inform you. Through fictional conversations between Roy Miller, our financial hero, and his barbershop patrons, you will learn that sound financial planning is not only relatively simple, but it can also be fun.

I wish you good reading and good planning.

David Chilton

1

THE FINANCIAL ILLITERATE

I love April. I wouldn't trade it for two of any other month. Except perhaps for October. Two Octobers would mean twice as many birthday presents — and Oktoberfests!

Why April? Weather-wise, it offers neither the best of summer nor the best of winter. It certainly doesn't provide the beauty of the fall months. Is it because, at least to poets and romantics, it symbolizes a new beginning, a kind of rebirth?

No.

I love April for three reasons: the National Basketball Association playoffs, the National Hockey League playoffs, and the essence of life itself — a new Major League Baseball season. Ah, April. Paradise on Earth!

Thanks to my convertor, I can sit motionless, flicking back and forth between the NBA on TSN and the NHL on CBC, while listening to my beloved Tigers winning on one radio and the despised Blue Jays losing on another. When you throw in a second TV and a VCR, the possibilities are endless.

In addition to being professional sports' finest hour, April also ushers in the start of the golf season and marks the return of Ontario's fastest-growing religion — slow-pitch.

Needless to say, my wife, Susan, is not quite as

fond of April as I am. However, even she would rank it among her favourite months. She is a fine tennis player, and April brings with it the first opportunity in half a year to hit the ball around. She also loves lawn work and spends a great deal of time in our garden. I use the word "our" loosely.

Surprisingly, slow-pitch season is something Susan enjoys as much as I do, if not more. The thirteen guys on our team range in age from twenty-eight to thirty-two, with me being the youngest. Seven are married and three have children. Tournaments, barbecues, pool parties, and evenings at our sponsor's — a terrific bar in Waterloo — are the highlights of the summer. All the wives and girlfriends get along famously. In fact, they appear to hold contests to see who can sit in the stands and pay the least attention to the game. Inevitably, when a game ends, the first thing our devoted fans ask is "Who won?"

This April, though, is a little different from Aprils gone by. Sue is pregnant, or as she likes to put it, "we" are pregnant. If it's true that we are pregnant, it is also true that I am handling it better than Sue. I am seldom tired and I haven't gained a single pound over the first five months.

Actually, Sue is handling the pregnancy very well. She is a beautiful woman who prides herself on her appearance, so she has kept in excellent shape. As for being tired, no way. She's too excited. I'm sure every woman feels that way when she's about to have a baby, especially her first, but Sue is in a different league. One week after our doctor's confirmation, she had completely furnished and decorated a nursery. We have also bought a complete set of encyclopedia. You never know when a child may feel a need to refer to an authority greater than his parent.

Our decision to have children was easy. Both Sue and I love kids. In a way, that's ironic because we both come from small families. Sue is an only child, and I have just one sibling. At thirty, my sister, Cathy, is two years older than I am, but because of our months of birth, she registered in school only one year before me. Much to everyone's surprise, I accelerated through grades three and four and caught up to her. This is something I have never let her forget.

As I said, deciding to have children was easy. Barring unforeseen events, we plan on having three. To be honest, I'd always hoped my first child would be a boy. But now that Sue is pregnant, all I'm hoping for is a healthy baby. Both families agree that, regardless of the baby's sex, it would be nice if the baby looked like Sue. Or, at the very least, didn't look like me.

Maybe I longed for a son because I thought that I would relate better to a boy and thus be a better parent. I asked my father if, way back oh so many years ago, he had hoped for a boy, and he replied, "Perhaps a little . . . but in hindsight two girls would have been nice." Sorry I asked!

Without a doubt, the highlight of the pregnancy to this point has been the reaction of the four first-time grandparents-to-be. Each excited couple phones at least once every forty-eight hours to see how Susan feels and to make sure I'm doing the housework and treating her well. This wouldn't bother me if it were only her parents questioning my abilities as a husband, but my parents are even worse. Dad says that Mom fainted when Susan told her I shampooed the rugs, and I'm not at all sure he's kidding.

Truthfully, helping with housework has been a great learning experience — not a great experience, but a great learning experience. I now know the origin of the expression "A woman's work is never done." My wife, for example, works as a travel agent from nine till five, comes home, cooks a meal, does laundry, and works out. I can understand why she always hits the sack at ten-thirty. I've been out like a light by nine since I reluctantly volunteered to do some of the household tasks.

I can't defend my previous lack of respect for housework. And I don't have to. It's my mother's fault. The wife of a high school principal, she has never held a paying job. As with most of their contemporaries, Dad brought home the bacon and Mom cooked it. While he was at work, Mom would do all the household chores, leaving her evenings free.

To my great pleasure, I was asked to do very little. While other kids mowed the lawn or shoveled snow, I chased down fly balls or played road hockey. I'm not sure why my parents were so easy on me, but to this day, I appreciate it.

On the other hand, Sue's parents, bucking the spoil-the-only-child stereotype, raised Sue to be a diligent worker. And to this day, I appreciate *that* even more! By the time we were married, she was used to doing housework and preparing meals. Being used to something, though, and enjoying it are far from synonymous. Now that I have come to realize just how much drudgery is involved in running a home, I am determined to become a *new and improved* person.

The guys on the slow-pitch team have started a pool, betting on how long the new me will last. Our pitcher informs me that the longest guess is four months — that is, until Sue is no longer pregnant. The shortest prediction, three weeks, was submitted by my wife. Now that's confidence.

As if taking it from the guys on the team two nights a week isn't bad enough, this weekend I'm going to get it from the future grandparents — live. As is our custom on the third weekend of each month, Sue and I are heading to Sarnia.

However, there's no need to feel sorry for us. Really. We go willingly. Both of us were born and raised there. Yes, it is an industrial town, and yes, it does have a distinct aroma. But Sarnia is not the grimy, run-down town non-Sarnians might imagine it to be — not at all. During my youth, its annual per capita income was consistently among the highest in Ontario. And believe me, the smoke and smell of the refineries are more than offset by the beauty of Lake Huron and the friendliness of the people.

If I seem defensive about Sarnia, it's because I am. In terms of diversification and growth potential, it certainly is no match for our current home, Kitchener. But there is something special about a hometown, especially one on the water. Sarnia comes alive in the summer. It's one continuous party, and to kids and teenagers that's pretty appealing.

In fact, that's pretty appealing to adults, too — us included. That's why this summer Sue and I are spending five weeks at a rented cottage just outside Sarnia, in Bright's Grove.

I've been teaching for four years now, and every summer I have either taken a course or taught one. But this year, with the baby due in early September, we elected to keep the summer open and head for the cool water.

Sue is ecstatic. There's a seasonal slowdown in the travel business, so, like me, she has July and August off every year. Her friends, however, do not. So those summers that I've been studying, working and golfing, she has often been forced to spend time alone, burning, peeling, and reading. I'm making it sound worse than it has been. As an independent woman, she has pursued several hobbies and interests. Nevertheless, she is really looking forward to seeing her two best friends and mother every day for five weeks this summer.

Initially, Sue's enthusiasm far outweighed mine. I have a great many friends in Sarnia, but only one of them is a teacher. Sure, Scott might be good for eighteen every morning — but who would I tee off with in the afternoons?

The more I thought about it, though, the more I warmed up to the idea. My best friend, Tom Garrett, is taking a holiday from his job at the refinery for the last three weeks of our stay. Tom loves to golf, go to Detroit Tiger games, lie on the beach, and quaff a few cold ones. In my book, the guy is perfect.

When Sue and I go to Sarnia for the weekend, we follow a fairly set routine.

We arrive Friday night at about eight-thirty. We usually go straight to my parents' house and enjoy a leisurely dinner. Then at ten-thirty, we go out to join some of our friends.

Saturday, Sue disappears. She does not save this act exclusively for Sarnia. In the four years we've been married, I've seen her only a dozen times on a Saturday afternoon — always at weddings. I'm not exactly sure where she goes, but it must be somewhere magical because invariably when she returns her shoes appear to have changed colour.

While she is AWOL — Absent with Our Loot — I spend the day with Tom. We meet my sister, Cathy, for breakfast at the Sarnia Golf Club at nine o'clock sharp. Depending on what we did Friday night after leaving my parents, this is sometimes not painless.

Tom and Cathy have a curious, combative relationship. They remind me of Maddie and David on "Moonlighting." They're always teasing and fighting, but it's obvious there's something there. As they're uninvolved and attractive people, it's surprising that they haven't at least tried going out together. But who am I to say? I thought Sonny and Cher were perfect for each other.

After breakfast, Cathy returns to her office to catch up on paperwork. She is the consummate Canadian success story. In grade 13, her average was 92 percent. Both Carleton and Western offered her generous scholarships. She decided that Western was perfect. It was close to Sarnia and had a prestigious school of medicine. My parents were calling her Dr. Richardson before we'd even left high school.

However, not only did Cathy not become a doctor, but she also didn't even go on to postsecondary education.

Knowing that her scholarship would cover most of her expenses, she felt no sense of urgency to get a summer job. Therefore, in the summer of grade 13, while I slaved at the refinery, Sis opened her own business. Combining her artistic flair with her love of horticulture, she founded Richardson Landscaping. The corporate name was simple, but the concept was pure genius.

Cathy spent the first four weeks of the summer combing the nicer neighbourhoods in Sarnia. When she spotted a property that she felt would look better if landscaped differently, she would do a series of sketches until she perfected "the look." While basking in the sun at the beach, she would do a watercolour of the final sketch.

The young entrepreneur would then frame the painting herself — tastefully, of course. A sticker on the back simply read, "This is how Richardson Landscaping sees your home." The framed picture was delivered, via courier, to the homeowner. The total cost to Cathy was approximately fifty dollars a picture.

Over the course of four weeks, she completed seventeen of these impressive and unique "business cards." At the end of the month, Cathy started following up with phone calls, and she booked an amazing fifteen appointments.

At this point, I was still far from impressed. Four

weeks into the summer, Cathy's venture was $850 in debt and I was constantly lending her money. As far as I knew, her scholarship did not include a recompense for her brother.

Within a few days, though, I was no longer worried. I was jealous!

Cathy's pitch during her appointments was, to use my students' favourite word, "awesome." For a flat fee of $1,000, she offered to gather tenders from four local landscaping firms, hire the appropriate choice, oversee all activities, and ensure that the job came in on time and on budget. There was no charge for her design.

Cathy's contagious enthusiasm, sound business proposal, and beautiful designs netted her six of the fifteen potential clients. Eleven years ago, $6,000 was an unbelievable summer job income!

She spent the rest of July and August supervising the six projects. Every customer was thrilled with the end result. Because she stayed on top of the land-scaping companies, jobs actually came in at prices substantially under the norm. In essence, her services paid for themselves.

Referrals started pouring in and she has never looked back. Last year, working only eight months, she made more money than my father and I combined.

At first, it was difficult to accept the fact that my sister, a university dropout before she even got there, was "a mover and a shaker." However, when I saw the type of Christmas and birthday gifts that success translated into, I became fiercely proud of her.

Despite her great achievement, Cathy is still a one-woman operation, preferring to handle all typing, billing, accounts payable, and other clerical duties herself — Saturdays.

That's all right with Tom and me, because she

wouldn't accompany us for the next item on our Saturday-in-Sarnia agenda, anyway. We go to the barber. That visit is one of the high points of the weekend. I'm sure most people don't think of a trip to the barber as a high point, but then again most people don't get their hair cut at Miller's Barbershop.

Roy Miller started giving us "buzz cuts" when we were five years old. We've outgrown that style, but remained true to Roy. In addition to being a very intelligent and witty fellow, he has the one quality that most endears a man to Tom and to me — he's a die-hard Tiger fan!

Like most barbers, Roy has a few Saturday regulars who are there only to pass the time. Two of the three, Jimmy and Clyde, don't have any hair left to cut. Clyde in particular gets a real kick out of our monthly visits. He is a big baseball fan, too — if you can be and cheer for the Blue Jays.

During the warm-weather months, the next item on Tom's and my itinerary is golfing. Both of us love the game, but despite being reasonably good athletes who have played golf for several years, neither of us excels at the sport. I have a fifteen handicap, while Tom's fluctuates between sixteen and twenty-two, depending on who's asking.

Saturday nights in Sarnia hold something different each month. Sometimes we assemble for a house party or a ball game. But most frequently, ten or fifteen of us descend on one of our favourite local watering holes.

Sundays, Sue and I go to church and out to brunch with her parents, whom I enjoy immensely. The Washburns have done quite well for themselves, owning and operating an industrial cleaning company. Like so many others, the company fell on tough times in the early eighties. Unlike so many others, owing in large part to my in-laws' work ethic and a debt-free balance sheet, it weathered the storm.

I wouldn't call them rich, but well-to-do wouldn't be pushing it. They have a new home on the lake, a cottage, a boat, and two nice cars. I don't think they have much in the way of investment assets, but because they have no debt, good cash flow, and a saleable business, their financial worries seem to be nonexistent.

After Sunday brunch, Sue and I head back to Kitchener. On the way out of town, we stop at Heaven's Gate Nursing Home. I still can't believe they named it that. Our only living grandparent, my grandmother, has been "waiting at the gate" for five years now. The doctors claim she is in excellent mental health, but I fear otherwise. She has developed the alarming habit of cheering for the Blue Jays.

Finally, we arrive back in Kitchener and spend Sunday evening recovering from the hectic weekend.

However, this upcoming weekend, our once-a-month routine will be slightly altered. On Friday, instead of going out after dinner, Sue and I are staying at my parents' so I can talk to my father. When I phoned him yesterday, I simply said that I needed to talk to him. I did not go into any details.

What a mistake! Mom called back five minutes later in hysterics. "Are Susan and the baby all right?" she demanded. "Are you all right? Did Cathy tell you something she hasn't told us? Are — "

To prevent my mother's impending coronary, I interrupted her barrage of questions and told her what I wanted to talk to Dad about — our finances.

Did it help? No. My mother persisted.

"Do you need money?" she continued shrilly. "Are you in trouble? Does this have to do with the time you — "

"No, Mom! I just need some basic financial planning advice."

"What led to this after all these years?" she asked skeptically. "What are you hiding from me?"

The fact is that when it comes to finances, I have nothing to hide. My lack of financial knowledge had really hit me for the first time just the other day. I was reading a local business publication when I stumbled across a "Self-Analysis Financial Planning Test."

No sweat, I thought. I'm a teacher. I don't fail tests; I fail students. Confidently, I picked up my pencil and set about responding to questions such as these:

- Have you selected the proper amortization period for your mortage?
- Is your will up-to-date?
- Could your dependants live comfortably in the event of your death?
- If you plan to retire early, have you set up a suitable savings program?
- How do you plan to pay for your children's education?
- Fifty percent of Canadians retire in financial hardship. What are you doing to guarantee you won't be one of them?
- Are your debts structured properly?

Not only could I not give a satisfactory answer to many of the questions, but also I didn't even understand some of them. I caught an ominous glimpse of Susan, our sons and me living as bag people.

I dropped my pencil, an unnerved man. It's not that I want to be a multimillionaire, though like everyone else, I do. I'll settle for being comfortable — very comfortable. I'd like to own a nice home and a cottage, help my children get an education, and retire in relative affluence at a reasonable age. And I want to accomplish all this without substantially sacrificing my present standard of living.

I think these goals are shared by most Canadians. Are they realistic? Can they be realized on an average salary? If so, how?

Within an hour of reading that article, I was committed to learning the basics of financial planning. I had no desire to learn the intricacies of the stock market, nor was it my goal to be able to recite mortgage tables from memory.

All I wanted to know was how best to get where I want to be from where I am now.

I figured Dad is no financial genius, but he must have learned a few things in his fifty-eight years. He seemed as good a place as any to start.

2
A SURPRISING REFERRAL

That April weekend trip to Sarnia changed my life.

* * *

The smell of my father's cigar, the voices of the Tiger radio announcers and talks about saving money rather than spending it do not rank high on Sue's list of favourite things. Throwing them all together proved to be too much for her. Claiming fatigue, she retired early that Friday night. My mother also bade us farewell — not to sleep, however, but to tackle the monthly chore of paying the bills.

Dad and I sat down to talk about something that in our twenty-eight years together we had never discussed before. In these days of open conversations about everything, including sexual habits, money remains a relatively taboo subject, even among family members. When you think about that, it's amazing!

"I can't believe we've never talked about money before," I marvelled.

"Even if we had, it would have been a short conversation," replied Dad. "Up until five years ago, I didn't know a thing about finances. Your mother and I lived from pay cheque to pay cheque, making our mortgage payments, staying out of debt, and sometimes saving for things we wanted. The only thing your grandparents really told me about money management was not to borrow.

"We couldn't teach you what we didn't know, and your grandparents couldn't teach us what they didn't know. I don't think it's our fault as a family. I suspect most people have the same problem, and I blame it partly on our education system.

"Five years ago, when I finally learned the basics of financial planning, I couldn't believe how straightforward they were. It's just common sense. If I had looked into the fundamentals thirty years ago, or even fifteen years ago, your mother and I would be very well off today."

"And I'd love you even more than I do now," I interjected. "But, Dad, for someone who didn't know much, you seem to have done all right."

"All right," he echoed, "but not great. And the frustrating part is that I now know great is achievable . . . easily achievable. It's incomprehensible to me that our government has not altered the school curriculum to include a basic family finance course. All high school graduates should know how to fill out an income tax form properly. They should know how to select their mortgage, how to finance their children's education, and how to save and plan for retirement.

"You know me, David. I've always believed that our country's education system is second to none, but that doesn't mean it can't use some improvement. There's no debating the fact that one of the most crucial improvements would be to teach basic money skills. Hell, we're raising generation after generation of financial illiterates. I don't think that even the politicians understand the tremendous benefits the economy would enjoy if Joe Average knew how to handle his money properly."

"Dad, why did you — "

"I can't believe Sparky is leaving Mike Henneman in

the game," Dad interrupted. "They're pounding him!" he added, as he rose to put the dog out.

As Dad left the room, I realized just how right he was. Sparky should have taken Henneman out.

He was also right about most Canadians being financial illiterates. There is no excuse for our possessing as little financial knowledge as we do. When even a university-educated person like me is embarrassed by an elementary financial test, something is wrong. Although I'd never thought about it before, Dad was also right about the fault lying with our education system. I teach history and geography, but I have to admit that being able to date the Battle of Hastings at 1066 is of little consequence compared to being able to create a proper savings program. Both forms of knowledge are important, and a balance must be found.

Dad reentered the room to a Mike Henneman game-ending strikeout. "Boy, is he a clutch pitcher, a great competitor," he said, beaming. "Big win, big win."

"How did you even manage to do 'all right' without knowing anything?" I continued.

"I'm not sure I like the way you phrased that," Dad replied with a laugh. "I brought home a fairly good income and we didn't have an extravagant lifestyle. God knows you never wanted for anything, but we had no investment assets at all. Often we didn't have any more than a couple of hundred dollars in the bank.

"Our only hard-and-fast rule was not to borrow. If we needed a new car, wanted to go on a trip, or had to put a new roof on the house, we would save the money first. If we didn't have anything specific on our 'wish list,' we spent our entire monthly income. That was our complete 'financial plan,' so to speak."

"You borrowed to buy the house, though?"

"Oh, yes, obviously, we had to borrow to buy the house. The trust company gave us a twenty-five-year mortgage that we finished paying off five years ago," Dad answered. "Actually, five years ago, a lot of things came together. We made our final mortgage payment. You were graduating, and except for not being able to make your own bed and cook, you were becoming self-sufficient. Our income increased significantly through my textbook sales, and your uncle died and left your mother $25,000."

"I didn't know that!" I exclaimed, surprised.

"You were at the funeral," Dad responded with a chuckle.

"No, no, not that Uncle George died. That he left Mom $25,000."

"We wanted to surprise you by leaving you more than just the house. You know, something to help you get over the inevitable trauma of losing the two greatest influences on your life."

"Yeah, yeah," I said, rolling my eyes.

"Anyway, when all those things happened at once, it became painfully obvious that I needed some financial advice. We had a couple of thousand dollars a month to play with and almost $27,000 sitting in the bank. I was ten years from retirement and both your mother and I figured we'd better seek professional help.

"I just didn't want to do something stupid. I knew that with my pension plan, my retirement looked pretty good. But I also knew that if I handled our new-found nest egg and our monthly surplus funds well, your mother and I could be looking at a cottage, a boat, some trips, or maybe even all these. Both of us had always wanted a place on the lake and this was our chance."

"So what did you do? Something intelligent, I hope, considering that someday all this could be mine."

"What about your sister? Don't you think it's only fair to leave her half?"

"Jackie Onassis? C'mon, Dad, it's pocket change for her," I joked. "What did you do?"

"I got the best haircut of my life," he deadpanned.

"Get serious, Dad. I really — "

"I am serious. I was down at Roy's one Saturday and I started talking to James Murray. You know James. . . . He's always there on Saturdays with Clyde and Jimmy."

"I know him well."

"Well, what you probably don't know is that before he became so successful selling real estate, he did stints as both a stockbroker and a life insurance agent. I told him I was in the market for some financial planning advice and asked him if he could recommend anyone. Even though he had been out of the field for about ten years, I figured he would still know someone competent.

"He smiled and said, 'The best financial planner in town is holding a razor at your throat.'"

"Roy? C'mon," I said, disbelieving.

"I'm not kidding and neither was James. Over the next several months, as he cut my hair, Roy taught me the basics of financial planning. And you'll be pleased to hear that right now my finances are in great shape, and they're looking better all the time."

"You're right. I am pleased to hear that. But how the heck does a barber become a financial planning expert?"

"The answer to that, and in fact Roy's background in general, is quite interesting. As you know, Roy and I were high school classmates. He was the all-American Canadian boy. You know what I mean . . . good-looking, athletic, bright, funny. Everybody liked Roy. He was our class valedictorian and was voted most likely to succeed.

"He had always talked about being a lawyer, so naturally he was Western-bound as a first step — "

"There are other universities, Dad," I interrupted.

"Only in your mind, son. Anyway, Roy and I lived in the same residence at university, but I didn't see him much. Between studying, playing varsity basketball and coming home to visit his girlfriend, he was a busy guy.

"In second year, five of us, including Roy, decided to rent a house. The first month was unbelievable. You know how it is. You aren't far enough into the courses to have papers or midterms, so you party every night. Remember all the things I told you not to do at university? Well, I was speaking from experience.

"Then, one night in early October, Roy got a phone call saying his father had died of a heart attack. By the next afternoon he had dropped out of school and moved back to Sarnia.

"His father, a fine man, had a history of heart problems. He had only worked at the refinery for ten years when he had his first heart attack. The doctors told him not to go back to physical work, but unfortunately he wasn't qualified for much else. To his credit, he didn't give up. Instead, he trained to become a barber and eventually opened Miller's Barbershop.

"Mrs. Miller worked as a maid during the day and as a waitress at night. Neither of them made a lot of money, but together they had enough to get by.

"When Mr. Miller died, Roy felt he had no choice but to quit school and go home to work. There was no way Mrs. Miller and Roy's younger sister, Ellen, could survive on a maid's pay. And like so many people, Mr. Miller hadn't carried enough life insurance.

"During high school, Roy had become a pretty darn good barber himself. He had learned the tricks of the trade from hanging around his father's shop. When his dad was really busy, Roy would cut hair to help out. In fact, in our first year at university, he cut hair in residence to make some extra money.

"When Roy had to return home from university, his game plan was simple. He was going to operate the barbershop until Ellen had completed college, and then he was going to sell it and go back to school. His sister was only in grade eleven at the time, so he was looking at about six years.

"We all felt bad about Roy having to put off his dream of becoming a lawyer, but deep down we knew he was doing the right thing. You've got to be there when your family needs you, even if it means personal sacrifice. You would do well to remember that, son, when your mother and I are old and want to move in with you."

"Don't even joke about that," I said in mock horror. "You still haven't explained how Roy became a financial planning expert. This isn't going to be one of your famous three-hour stories, is it?"

"No, no. I'm getting to the financial part.

"Roy did a tremendous job running the barbershop. He did some things that at the time were unique. Without a doubt, the most innovative and profitable was 'the hair truck.' Apart from the Tigers, Roy has always had two main hobbies. One is going to auctions and the other is tinkering with old cars and trucks. In his second year at the shop, he combined the two hobbies beautifully.

"He bought a barber chair at an auction and installed it in the back of an old moving truck. Then he put in a basin complete with running water, a power supply, and even a magazine rack. On Tuesdays, Roy took the hair truck to the refineries. He lifted the sliding door on the back and, voilà, he was open for business. The workers flocked over during their breaks and lunches. . . . It was so convenient. What was the worst day of the week for most barbers was now Roy's best. In fact, he did so well on

Tuesdays that he hired another barber to go back on Wednesdays and Thursdays. Eventually, a new by-law put a stop to all the fun. But in the four or five years the hair truck was in operation, Roy brought in a lot of business and, more important, built a large and loyal clientele.

"He wasn't making a corporate lawyer's wage, but he was doing well, very well . . . We've never discussed what we make, but I would think our incomes over the years have been quite similar."

"What happened to the six-year plan?" I asked.

"Roy loved being a barber. It's as simple as that. To this day, he loves working downtown, dealing with people, owning his own business, all of it. It's funny, but Roy has really lived up to his most-likely-to-succeed billing. I don't know a more successful, well-rounded person."

"What about the financial planning part, Dad? I have to be home by Sunday, you know."

"I'm getting there, I'm getting there. Roy was really shaken by the poor financial shape his mother had been left in. His father had had no pension, no savings, and very little insurance. Roy laughs now when he says the only thing his father left them was a mortgage, but it wasn't funny at the time.

"He vowed not to make the same mistakes. Yet after a couple of years running the shop and making a good income, Roy had very little to show for his efforts. His mother and sister were being well taken care of, but financially that was about it.

"Roy decided it was time to do something. He started reading everything he could on money management. At that time, almost all financial books concentrated on investment alternatives, not on mundane topics like saving, buying a house, and insurance — you know, the common person's concerns. They all showed what to do with money once you had it, but they didn't tell you how to accumulate it.

"However, Roy's father had always told him that if you want to learn to do something right, watch someone who does it successfully. Roy reasoned that that certainly held true for sports, so it probably held true for just about everything else, too, including financial planning.

"So at the age of twenty-three, Roy did what he now calls the smartest thing he has ever done. He went to visit Maurice White.

"Old Mr. White was one of the wealthiest men in town. He owned a jewellery store, a huge farm, several race horses, and half the real estate downtown. Included in those holdings was the building that housed Miller's Barbershop.

"Mr. White had always liked Roy. He admired him for his loyalty to his family and he was also quite impressed with Roy's entrepreneurial approach to increasing business. When Roy told Mr. White why he had dropped by, Mr. White nodded. 'You've come to the right place, my lad. I'll teach you *the golden secret* of financial success in one hour.'

"Well, David, that was quite an hour. I venture to say there aren't many barbers who started with nothing and today own a beautiful house on the lake, a large investment portfolio, an office building, and have their retirement well taken care of."

"All that from just one secret? What was it?" I asked eagerly.

"Slow down. It's not that simple. Roy continued to read and learn about financial planning. His knowledge of insurance, RRSPs and investments has really helped him. But there's no doubt that hour was the catalyst. I'm not telling you any more, though. Roy teaches financial planning better than anyone, and I know he'll be more than happy to share his knowledge with you. In fact, I've already told him you won't just be talking about the Tigers tomorrow."

"I'm not sure I'll be able to follow him," I responded, feeling worried. "I don't understand all those fancy money terms, and as you may remember, math was never my strong suit."

"As I said earlier, son, it's just common sense. You'll be astonished when you learn how easy it is to handle your finances properly. If you listen to Roy, you'll never have any financial worries. You'll be so wealthy you'll be able to build your mother and me a guest house down in Kitchener."

"I'm not sure I want to be wealthy, after all," I said, slapping his shoulder affectionately.

* * *

"Boy, are you tanned!" I complimented Cathy, over breakfast. "It's only April and you're mahogany."

"Hanging out at the tanning studios?" Tom asked. "Man, that's an expensive habit. How much do those sessions cost?"

"Well, uh, I haven't been going to the studios. I bought my own tanning machine," an embarrassed Cathy replied.

"Must be nice! I slave all day at the plant to make ends meet and you're buying your own electric beach! If you'd just work on your personality a bit, I'd ask you to marry me."

"What if one of the girls you asked last night at the bar says yes? Bigamy is illegal, you know, Tom," Cathy pointed out.

"Oh, Tom," I groaned, "you weren't using that stale line again? What happened to 'Excuse me, miss, can I buy you a Porsche?'"

"Gimme a break, you two! To meet women, a man's gotta do what a man's gotta do. Besides, that Porsche line has served me pretty well over the years."

"Well, I think it's running out of gas," Cathy teased.

"Did you really buy a tanning machine, Sis?"

"Yeah. I had some extra money and I love being dark. Besides, it didn't cost all that much."

"I'll bet," I said sarcastically. "What do you do with all your money? You must own half of Sarnia by now."

"Hardly. With my car payments, mortgage payments, condo fees, credit cards, and daily living expenses, there's hardly anything left."

"Tough life, baby," Tom sighed. "You really should apply for some sort of government aid. SISIM or something — Supplemental Income for Single Independent Millionairesses."

"How can you party so hard at night and still be so witty in the morning, Tom? It never ceases to amaze me. Anyway, the truth is, I've blown my money pretty badly. Except for my down payment, my furnishings, and a small RRSP, I haven't saved much at all. I get calls all the time from brokers and insurance agents who want to give me advice, but I distrust insurance agents and I don't understand a thing brokers say."

"Talk about perfect timing. You won't believe the conversation I had with Dad last night! That's why I didn't go out. I wanted to discuss financial planning. With Sue and me about to have a baby, I want to start investigating things. We're looking for a house now; I'll need insurance, a college education fund for Davey, Jr. — all that stuff."

"Davey, Jr.? You must be kidding," Tom scoffed between mouthfuls of his tenth piece of toast.

"So what did Dad say? I didn't know he knew anything about money."

"He didn't until five years ago. Then he learned the basics of financial planning and now he says he's in great shape. I'll tell you something. You guys won't believe who taught him — Roy Miller."

"What the hell does Roy know about financial planning?" Tom demanded.

"A lot. You know how we figured Roy's wife must have inherited some pretty big money? Uh uh. It turns out the house, the BMW, the boat — everything — were all earned through good financial planning. Roy started from scratch and with only average earnings turned himself into one wealthy barber."

"How?"

"I don't know yet, but you can bet I'm going to find out. In fact, our favourite barber is going to start teaching me this morning. Dad says Roy will teach me all I need to know to gain financial peace of mind."

"That sounds great. Do you two mind if I tag along today?" Cathy asked hopefully. "I don't need a shave — but I do need the advice."

"No, come on along," I invited her. "Who knows? Maybe one Saturday years from now we'll be eating brunch on the Mediterranean, remembering this as the most important morning of our lives."

"The wealthy barber," Tom muttered, shaking his head.

|3|
THE WEALTHY
BARBER

When we arrived at Roy's, he was just finishing up
Mr. Thacker's shave, if you can call it a shave. I don't
think Mr. Thacker has had any facial hair growth
since he turned ninety, five years ago.

"How are you, Johnny?" Mr. Thacker inquired,
looking me straight in the eye.

"I'm Dave."

"Sorry, Dan. I always get you confused with your
brother."

"I don't have a brother, Mr. Thacker. You're thinking of — "

"Dear me, what happened to your brother? The
poor boy couldn't have been more than thirty!"

"I never had a brother. You're thinking of — "

"Oh, yes, I'm sorry. I thought you were one of the
Richardson boys, the principal's sons."

I wasn't at all sure how to proceed at this point,
but before I had a chance to decide, Mr. Thacker had
started for the door.

"The old boy's getting a bit senile, eh, Roy?" I
sympathized, after the door had closed.

"Are you kidding, Davey? He knew who you were
the whole time. It's all an act. He figures I won't ask
him to pay if I think he's losing it."

"So do you make him pay?" asked Tom.

"Sure do. If I gave a free cut to every weirdo who

25

came in, I'd be broke in a month, and you two boys wouldn't have paid in years.

"Nice tan, Cathy!" Roy commented before returning his attention to me. "Hey, Dave, did you see the article in the *Observer* last Wednesday on the female Midas here?"

Roy was referring to a full-page feature in the local paper that made my sister sound like the smartest and most talented woman alive.

"My mother showed it to me," I answered. "Five times."

"If you want to make it six, it's on the bottom of my birdcage," Tom injected with a chuckle.

I myself didn't find that line particularly funny, but it got a couple of knee slaps from Jimmy, who was reading the paper in the corner.

"Hey, where's Clyde?" I wondered.

"He's on holidays," James Murray informed me, "down in Florida at his sister's. I heard it was ninety-eight degrees down there yesterday. He'll be on a liquid diet for sure."

At this point I hopped up into Roy's chair. I always go before Tom, who insists on making sure Roy is "on" before he'll go near him.

"I was talking to my father last night about financial planning. With Sue and me about to buy a house and have a baby, I figured it's time I learn a few things. Dad told me you know more about financial planning than anybody, so Cathy, Tom, and I are hoping you can teach us the basics."

"Your father mentioned on Thursday that he was going to recommend you talk to me. Like I told him, I'd be more than happy to help out. He came to see me five years ago himself, and we put him on the right track."

"So I heard. That's good news. But he had some money to invest. I'm not sure you'll be able to do much for me. The only money Sue and I have is what we've saved for our down payment."

"Dave, investing and financial planning are not synonymous. Financial planning is really nothing more than the proper handling of cash flow and assets to meet your objectives. Oh, there are wills and insurance and a few other things, and we'll talk about all that later, but basically, how you handle your income and assets will determine your success.

"Let's be honest. Most young people don't have any assets, except maybe a home. So it comes down to managing your cash flow."

"You mean budgeting?" I queried. "I'm terrible at that."

"No, I don't mean budgeting. Everybody's terrible at that. Very few people have become financially successful through budgeting, and the ones who have aren't much fun at parties."

"Ho, ho," Cathy piped up. "So if we don't budget, how do we save money? I sure never have any left at the end of the month. I spend everything. The better business gets, the more I spend."

"Let's not get ahead of ourselves here. I admire your enthusiasm, but let's slow down a bit.

"I can make all three of you financially successful. I've done it for lots of people, these clowns included," Roy said, nodding at Jimmy and James. "Starting next month, each time you come in, I'll teach you a different part of a solid financial plan. Seven months from now, you'll be on the road to prosperity, and you'll tell everyone that Roy Miller is the greatest man who ever lived."

"We already tell people that, Roy," Tom said, smiling.

"How can you teach us so much in so little time? I mean, Roy, you really are working with novices. Tom and Dave and I are financial idiots!"

"Cathy, my job will be removing the word *financial* from that statement. You'll have to worry about the other part yourselves. Trust me . . . Good financial planning is nothing more than common sense. The old KISS philosophy at its best. Keep It Simple . . . Sarnians.

"We all share pretty much the same goals — an annual vacation, a nice car, a comfortable home, a cottage, early retirement, the ability to give our children what they need and want . . . and baseball season's tickets. These are the average Canadian's goals.

"And I'll tell you right now, they're easily attainable . . . easily. Especially if you start young. Time is your greatest ally. If you three start now, I guarantee you that you will exceed all your goals — dramatically.

"Look at me. I'm a barber, for crying out loud! I'm proud of my business, but I'm the first to admit that I'm not pulling in a doctor's salary. Far from it. Yet you'd be hard-pressed to find many professionals with better financial statements than mine. I hope it doesn't sound like I'm bragging. It's just that it's important for you to know that if someone as simple as me can become wealthy, it's certainly possible for you geniuses."

"You're not simple, Roy. Maybe a bit slow, but not simple," Tom wisecracked.

"I don't want to seem cynical, Roy, but if it's so easy, why isn't everyone doing it?" I asked.

"Lack of knowledge. Your dad and I talk about this all the time. Our schools don't teach money skills. Our family members don't talk money. And just as important, there are very few places for an aspiring learner to turn. Our financial industry is geared toward product sales, not toward dispensing well-rounded financial planning advice.

"Most insurance agents sell cash-value policies;

mutual fund salespeople sell funds and tax shelters; brokers sell stocks and bonds; bankers sell guaranteed investment certificates, and so on and so on. You can't blame them. Product sales are where the money is, so very few of them are true *financial planners*."

"Are there any good product-oriented financial planners?" I asked.

"Sure there are, but none can do as well for you as you can do for yourself if you're well-informed."

Tom looked quizzical. "What about fee-only planners?"

"Don't depend too much on financial planners," Roy replied emphatically. "Learn for yourself. Nobody cares as much about your money as you do. You have to take responsibility for your own future. As I said earlier, the great thing is, it's not hard."

"Dad said last night that some old guy taught you a golden secret when you were young. What is it?" I probed.

"Oh, no. I'm saving that for next month. If you only pay attention once in the next seven months, let it be next month. If you follow that lesson, even if you do everything else poorly, I guarantee you that someday you'll be rich."

"Can't we start today?" I implored.

"No," to my chagrin, was his firm answer. "My granddaughter's going to be here in five minutes. I'm taking care of her for the afternoon. Cathy can stay, but I want you two out of here ASAP. Emily's only three years old, and I don't want to scare her off men for the rest of her life."

Never before had I been tempted to get my hair cut two consecutive weeks. Roy had really piqued my interest. I've known him all my life and he has always come across as a very modest man. The matter-of-fact confidence he displayed when discussing Tom's, Cathy's and my financial futures was out of character — and contagious. There was no doubt in my mind that I had taken the first step along the road to financial prosperity.

▌4▐
THE TEN-PERCENT
SOLUTION

I can't remember a rainstorm worse than the one that occurred on the third Saturday in May. A north wind had come up and was blowing at seventy kilometers an hour. That, combined with a torrential downpour, had caused most Sarnians to stay inside. Most smart Sarnians, that is.

There was no way Tom, Cathy and I were going to miss out on the golden secret. We had been looking forward to it for a month. We were so excited that we even skipped breakfast.

As usual, I drove. My parents' house has indoor access to the garage and both Tom and Cathy have underground parking, so, surprisingly, it was possible to remain perfectly dry until we arrived at the shop. On the way there, Cathy suggested that Roy might be closed because of the weather. Tom and I just laughed. Roy hasn't missed an entire day of work in thirty-seven years for any reason. He had even opened on the morning of his daughter's wedding.

With so few people venturing out, we were able to get the parking spot right in front of Miller's. Between our umbrellas and his awning, we managed to get from the car to the shop door relatively undrenched.

It was locked.

Clyde, with his Florida tan, was standing on the other side peering out through the glass. "All you have to do is say 'We love the Blue Jays,' and I'll let you in. We've got coffee brewing," he chirped in his reedy voice.

By this time, we were starting to get pretty wet. And annoyed. The angle of the rain was such that it was impossible to protect ourselves anymore, even with the help of the awning and umbrellas.

"I love the Blue Jays!" Cathy cried, not amused.

Traitor. Tom and I stood stoically.

Clyde shook his head and let all of us in. "You boys really are die-hards. You should seek professional help."

"You telling us we need a psychiatrist is like Karl Malden telling someone she needs a nose job," Tom murmured, as he towelled off.

"I thought you three might not show. It's terrible out there," Roy commented.

"What? And miss our long-awaited, eagerly antic-ipated first lesson? You've got to be kidding!" I re-torted. "What I can't believe is that these three have shown up in this weather," I added, motioning to-ward Clyde, Jimmy, and James Murray. I'm not sure why I always use James Murray's given and family names. Perhaps it's because when I was young I thought his name was James-Murray, like Billy-Bob or Bobby-Joe.

"They wouldn't miss free coffee and doughnuts if we had a tornado. You should know that by now," Roy replied, as he straightened up the counter.

"Roy, I've been looking forward to today for a month. My financial situation is getting worse in-stead of better," Cathy began impatiently. "I can hardly wait to hear what you have to say."

"Okay, let's get started. As your father has proba-bly told you, I took over this shop thirty-odd years ago when my dad died. I got lucky and a few of my ideas paid off. After a couple of years, I was making a pretty good income. Very good for a barber. I added a couple of chairs in the other room, and all in all, things were moving along well.

"I decided to make barbering my life's work. I knew my income from the shop was respectable, but it was never going to make me a rich man. That bothered me because, frankly, I wanted to be wealthy. I grew up poor, and believe me, poverty is something you don't acquire a taste for. I didn't want to live in town in a tiny one-bedroom home — I wanted to live on the lake. I wanted to own this building, too. I wanted a nice car, trips to Europe, and some of the other fine things life has to offer.

"The only way I could accomplish all that on my income was to budget and save like a madman. Or at least that's what I thought. So I developed a budget — so much for rent, so much for food, so much for clothes, so much for savings . . . you know. Two years after starting to budget, I had very little to show for it. Sure enough, at the end of each month I'd end up saying, 'So much for savings,' but unfortunately it didn't mean what I had hoped it would mean. It was pretty depressing.

"Like you, Dave, I realized I didn't know anything about financial planning, and it was high time to learn. I didn't have a father to turn to, so I went to a person who I figured must know a lot about money, he had so much — old Mr. White.

"I explained my situation to him. I told him what I wanted to achieve. 'Is it possible?' I asked.

"He told me, 'Wealth beyond your wildest dreams is possible if you learn the golden secret: *Invest ten percent of all you make for long-term growth.* If you follow that one simple guideline, someday you'll be a very rich man.'"

"That's it?" asked Tom. "I could have gotten that from a Bank of Nova Scotia commercial!"

"Patience, Tom," replied Roy. "Patience. I felt the same way myself. I wasn't very impressed when Mr.

White told me, either. My budget was already designed to save even more than ten percent, and at that point, it wasn't working and I was far from wealthy. But Mr. White went on to explain a few things that I'll tell you now, things that turn a seemingly simple sentence into an extremely powerful thought.

"Cathy, if you invested $2,400 a year, say $200 a month, for the next thirty years, and averaged a fifteen percent return a year, how much money do you think you'd end up with?" challenged Roy.

"Well, $2,400 times thirty is $72,000."

"I'm impressed," I interrupted.

"... plus growth... I don't know... I'd say $200,000. Maybe not quite that much," Cathy concluded.

"Wrong. The answer is $1.4 million," Roy declared.

"Get real!" was Tom's initial reaction. When he realized that Roy was serious, he paled. "What about inflation? And where am I going to get fifteen percent? For that matter, where am I going to get $200 a month?" he stammered.

"All good questions, Tom, and we'll get to them in due course. Dave, you try one. If you had started putting thirty dollars a month away, the equivalent of a dollar a day, at age eighteen and you continued until age sixty-five, averaging a fifteen percent annual return, how much would you end up with?"

"I hate math, Roy, but I'll give it a shot. Thirty dollars a month is $360 a year, times forty-seven years . . . Anybody have a calculator?"

"It's just under $17,000," injected Roy.

"Plus growth. I'll say about $70,000."

"Close," responded Roy. "The answer is approximately $2,000,000!"

"Bull," scoffed Tom, as if he had read my mind.

"No, not bull . . . magic. The magic of compound interest — interest on principal and interest, not just simple interest on principal. The eighth wonder of the world. Thirty dollars a month, a dollar a day, will magically turn into around two million. And do you know what's even more impressive? You know someone who has done it," Roy said proudly.

"Thirty-five years ago, I started my savings with thirty dollars a month, which was approximately ten percent of my earnings. I have achieved just under a fifteen percent average annual return. In addition, as my income rose, my ten percent saving component rose accordingly. Thirty dollars a month became sixty dollars, then a hundred, and eventually hundreds of dollars a month.

"You three are looking at a very wealthy man."

"Are you trying to tell us that by saving ten percent of every pay cheque you've turned yourself into a millionaire?" an intense Tom demanded.

"Precisely" was the incredible response.

Roy Miller, a millionaire! I sat stunned. I knew he had done well, but a millionaire? To the best of my knowledge, I'd never met a millionaire, and I sure didn't expect my first to be my barber. Roy was clearly deriving great pleasure from the disbelief on our three faces.

"Compound interest . . . mind-boggling, isn't it?" he went on. "When the Indians sold Manhattan to the Dutch for beads worth twenty-four dollars, it seemed like the natives got taken. But if they had invested that money at eight percent interest, today their tribe would be worth trillions of dollars."

"Have you ever thought about buying Manhattan, Roy?" Cathy teased.

"It's a real tragedy that most people don't understand compound interest and its wondrous powers. Take your dad, David. If he had started his program at the same time I did, you'd be looking at a big inheritance down the road."

"You still haven't answered my questions about the effects of inflation, where we get fifteen percent, and how we save two hundred a month. Hell, I'm lucky to save two hundred a year, and even if I could save money, I don't know anything about investing — the stock market, options, commodities . . . C'mon, Roy, you've got to be kidding!"

Tom's points were well taken. Saving money is never easy. No one — and I mean no one — has devoted more time to developing a budget than Susan and I. Yet every month, apart from our down-payment fund, we don't manage to save a cent. As for investing, the only investment I've ever made was a stock on the Vancouver exchange. I lost $1,000 in one week. A thousand dollars I couldn't afford to lose. A thousand dollars that was needed for my tuition.

"I'll talk about saving and investing in a minute," Roy commenced. "As for inflation, well, I'm sure that, in the mid-fifties, people probably said, 'Yeah, saving ten percent sounds like a good idea, but what's a couple of million going to be worth in the eighties, anyway?' Sure, inflation is going to have an impact. But not a devastating one. Far from it. In fact, inflation is all the more reason to save. Things are going to get more expensive. Lakefront properties are going to continue to rise in price. Jaguars are going to cost more. But believe me, if you save ten percent, you'll be parking your XJ6 beside your cottage some-day. Remember that your wages will continue to rise, too, as will your ten percent saving. My original ten percent stake was only thirty dollars a month; yours will be much more, and so will your total wealth. That will do a lot to offset inflation. If you handle your savings wisely, your growth rate should far exceed the inflation rate. Maybe not every year, but certainly on average.

"It's the person who doesn't save ten percent who has to worry about inflation, not the person who does," he summarized.

"So how do we earn fif — "

"Slow down, slow down. Let's talk about saving the money first. When people think about saving, they think about budgeting. I'll allot so much of my income for this, so much for that, et cetera, et cetera, and at the end of the month, I'll have so much left over. But as each of us knows all too well, something goes wrong. Money keeps running out before the month does.

"You know, it's funny. When I took over the shop, it was obvious that cost management hadn't been one of my father's strengths. I designed a detailed budget that covered all my potential expenses. I stuck to it like glue. That budget played a major part in my early success. To this day, I still do a shop budget once a year. And I still stick to it.

"After a couple of years running the shop, I couldn't understand how my personal budget could be such a waste of time, while my business budget worked like a charm. I discussed the situation with old Mr. White. I'll never forget his reply. 'Roy, my young friend,' he said, 'a business only has to budget for needs. It's in the best interest of the business to limit those needs as much as possible. An individual, on the other hand, must budget for both needs and wants. It is a rare person who can do that successfully because, for too many people, *a want becomes a need.*'

"And it's so true! Did I need a new car in my second year of business, or did I just want one? Cathy, did you need to get away to Europe last winter, or did you just want to? Tom, did you need, or just want, the best stereo available? It's human nature to spend our entire disposable income and to rationalize all those expenditures as needs."

"Good point, Roy, but you have to have some fun, too. One of the reasons I make money is to spend it on things I like," I argued.

"Young people of all generations think alike, Dave.

That's exactly what I said to Mr. White. Remember, I grew up poor. The first time I'd ever had any fun money was during my first couple of years at the shop. 'No one is trying to tell you to squirrel away every cent, Roy,' Mr. White explained. 'But if you want to accomplish your goals, you must save something. I think you can see that. Luckily, there's an almost painless way to save, a way to save where you barely notice the money has gone!'"

"I might not know much about financial matters,'" Tom blurted out, "but I know there's no painless way to save . . . no way, nohow."

A voice sounded from the corner of the room. "Be quiet and listen."

The source of that remark really caught me off guard. In the twenty-odd years I had known him, Clyde had not said one serious thing. And that's not an exaggeration. That he was even paying attention to such a no-nonsense conversation was startling, let alone that he seemed eager for it to continue.

"Clyde," Roy asked mischievously, "is there a painless way to save?"

"Sure is. *Pay yourself first.* Old Mr. White knew what he was talking about when he told you that," Clyde said with a nod.

"Oh, no," Tom muttered. "Don't tell me Billy Blue Jay over there is rich, too. The wealthy barber I can take, but the wealthy wacko . . . that's too much!'"

Roy and Clyde just grinned at each other.

"Pay yourself first. I can't tell you what those three little words have meant to me," Roy reflected. "After agreeing that the ad hoc approach to saving doesn't work, and after explaining to me why the budgeting approach seldom works, Mr. White announced that the only way to save is to pay yourself first. Although he was talking about saving the ten percent, the axiom holds true for all savings. Whether you're saving for a down payment, a car, a trip, whatever, the most effective thing is to have the money come right off your pay cheque, or right out of your bank — *before you have a chance to spend it*. But we'll talk more about saving for those kinds of items in a few months.

"Anyway, I was a bit skeptical at first. I was helping my mom and sister get by, paying my shop's rent, making car payments and trying to save for both a down payment and an engagement ring. And I wasn't meeting with much success. In my mind, there was no way I could set aside an additional ten percent. Where was I going to get that thirty dollars a month? There was nothing left at the end of the month as it was. I had tried budgeting and that hadn't worked. Then Mr. White made a very generous offer. 'Roy, you arrange to have that thirty dollars a month go directly into a separate bank account and from there to an investment. If at any time saving that thirty dollars runs you short of funds, I'll lend you whatever you need at no interest. You can pay me back whenever it's convenient for you.'

"How could I say no? Anyway, I never did miss that money. My lifestyle didn't change at all. I know thirty dollars doesn't sound like much now, but remember it was ten percent of my income back then, and I never missed it.

"But the best example I've ever seen of the pay-yourself-first rule not adversely affecting someone's life is Clyde.

"Good pension at work, lived in an apartment, no wife, no kids, no debt that was Clyde fifteen years ago. Actually, that's Clyde today, too. In the mid-70s, Clyde told me he had his eye on a gorgeous $20,000 sailboat he'd love to have for retirement. You could get a heck of a boat fifteen years ago for twenty grand. I reminded Clyde, though, that by the time he retired, thanks to inflation, that boat would cost a pretty penny more. The only way he would be able to afford it would be to start putting aside money right away. We started him on a couple of hundred a month . . . a big chunk of his income back then. 'I'll never survive,'" Roy mimicked. "'I won't be able to go out at all. I'll have to go Dutch on my dates.'

"Clyde was convinced bankruptcy was just around the corner. Four months after we started the saving program, I asked him how he was struggling along without the $200 a month. He said, 'Geez, I'd forgotten all about that.'

"The significance of that reply can't be overstated. He'd forgotten he was even doing it! Over the years I've taught dozens of people the pay-yourself-ten-percent-first rule. Not one has noticed a dramatic change in his or her standard of living . . . until they're sipping martinis on their boats, that is," Roy reported with a satisfied grin.

"Ask your dad, Dave. He'll tell you. It really is amazing. You know how quickly you adjust to your raises? Well, this is pretty much the same thing, but in reverse."

"I don't make a lot of money and I didn't start saving until fifteen years ago. But today, I'm not only looking at a boat, but I'm looking at a pretty darn good retirement overall. If you three start at your age, the sky's the limit." Clyde beamed as he gave Tom an encouraging pat on the back.

"I want to make something clear here," Roy proceeded. "At different times in your life, you're going to have to save for various things — a house, a car, a trip, whatever. A house, in particular, is a major expenditure. There is no way to achieve some goals without sacrificing your current standard of living . . . I mean, let's be realistic. But the ten percent saving is different. It's regular. It's a constant. You don't even see it. It comes right off your pay cheque or out of your bank. You won't believe how easy that makes it."

"I can see that saving ten percent of your income shouldn't be too hard, especially if you pay yourself first. But I'm still curious about those fifteen percent rates of return," Tom persisted. "Last time I looked at my savings, which I admit are pitiful, they were earning a paltry six percent."

"Achieving higher rates of return over the long run is simple." Roy shrugged. "Be an owner, not a loaner."

"C'mon, Roy, I don't know anything about owning stocks or gold or real estate," Tom protested. "Hell, I saw what the market did in October '87. I want no part of that."

"Tom, you missed four key words — 'over the long run.' Ownership, at least ownership governed by common sense, will always outperform loaning in the long run. It has to. If it were consistently more profitable for businesses and individuals to leave their money in the bank than to invest it in North American enterprises, we'd all be in big trouble. Eventually, our whole economic system would collapse. That won't happen. And in the unlikely event that it were to, it wouldn't do you any good to have your money sitting down at the bank . . . because the banks would all be locked." Roy laughed.

"You see, despite all the bitching and complaining and occasional difficult economic times, opportunities will always exist for clear-thinking individuals. VCRs, microwaves, gas barbecues . . . your parents didn't enjoy perks like that when they were young. Technological advances, medical discoveries, social programs . . . Do I have to go on? The fact is, we're living in great times. If you're healthy and living in Canada, you have very little to complain about, apart from the Blue Jays.

"I know we've got acid rain, deficits, unemployment problems in the East, and so on. And these are serious problems. Unfortunately, we'll always have serious problems. But the majority of them will eventually be solved. 'It is a gloomy moment in history. Not in the lifetime of any man who reads his paper has there been so much grave and deep apprehension . . . The United States is beset with racial, industrial and commercial chaos, drifting we know not where . . . and Russia hangs like a storm cloud on the horizon . . . Of our troubles, no man can see the end.'

"Quite an editorial, don't you think? It was written in *Harper's* magazine. Do you know when? In *1847!* I think you get my point.

"I believe that the next twenty to thirty years will present some of the greatest opportunities ever. So much change. So many things happening. The only way to be a part of it all and to share in the successes is through ownership."

"So should we buy common stocks?" I asked.

"No, with your ten percent savings, common stocks are not the way to go" was Roy's solemn warning.

Needless to say, this caught me by surprise. "You've never owned a common stock?" I questioned.

"Never. I don't know anything about stock analysis, and I don't have any friends who do, either. It's a tough game. You have to be disciplined. To perform well, you have to buy when everyone else is selling and sell when everyone else is buying, using a rare combination of guts and brains. You have to have a good background in economics and you have to use that background to look into the future. You not only have to see the various companies' management teams, but you also have to know what questions to ask them. Most of all, you have to have a sixth sense, an intuition, a knack of recognizing value. Very few people fill the bill. I certainly don't. I mean, think about it. Do you know anybody who's become rich buying and selling stocks? There aren't many. It's just too difficult."

"What about using stockbrokers? They must know what they're doing," I asserted.

"I was a stockbroker for several years, Dave," James Murray noted, "and I can assure you that when it comes to picking and choosing stocks, a broker is usually no better than the next guy. A comedian once said, 'A broker is someone who invests your money until you have none.' I think a more accurate line may be, 'A broker is someone who invests your money until it's his.'"

"They're around stocks all day; they must know something."

"Dave, they're salespeople. That's it. Instead of selling shoes or beds, they're selling stocks. They spend all day on the phone talking to clients, reading research reports, looking at undecipherable financial statements. In the five years I was a broker, only one guy in our office turned a profit in his personal trading account in any calendar year. One!"

"You?"

"Me? I was the worst! I thought I was a hotshot because I was driving a fancy car, eating at pricey restaurants and taking home a hefty cheque. Unfortunately, I couldn't have consistently picked winning stocks if my life had depended on it.

"After five years, I got disgusted and quit. My commissions were great but my clients' investment performance was dismal. It hit me hard when I realized it's all a game. You know what still bothers me? Most of my clients were really happy with me. I gave excellent service, was nice on the phone, threw good cocktail parties, and knew all the right things to say. I know I could have remained a prosperous broker for years, losing people's money the whole time.

"One guy in our office was nearing retirement when I came aboard. He'd been a broker for thirty years, and was very well thought of. When he retired to his summer home and yacht, his accounts were divvied up. I got ninety of them, some very good. I started examining what he had been doing for the clients so I'd be well informed when I called to introduce myself. I'll never forget it. Of ninety accounts, only seven were up money over the years, and only one of those was up dramatically."

"Why do people stay with their brokers if they constantly lose money?" Cathy queried.

"Who knows? Some don't stay. They switch to other brokers, who often also end up losing them money. Others don't care, because they play the market for excitement more than profit. And I know this sounds hard to believe, but I'm convinced that many don't even know whether they're up or down.

"I remember one client that had been dealing with the retiring broker for fifteen years. He had started with $50,000 and fifteen years later, he had $55,000. 'That's better than a loss,' he said. He didn't understand that if he had just left the money in the bank, he would have had substantially more than $55,000. Like so many others, he didn't understand compound interest.

"A major reason people lose money with their brokers is that they constantly go against the wisdom of *let your profits run and cut your losses*. Most investors and brokers cut profits and let losses run.

"Good investors admit their mistakes and sell, taking small losses. Those losses are easily covered by the large profits created through a combination of buying value and exercising patience . . . Patience that most of us don't have.

"Bad investors always think their stocks are going to come back up to at least what they cost them. Brokers know they look bad when they choose a loser, so rather than selling and accepting a loss, they perpetuate this myth. A stock doesn't know you own it — it's not going back to twenty-two so you can get out even. So you often end up holding as the stock goes lower and lower."

"James, are you saying brokers are dishonest?" Cathy probed.

"No, no . . . I didn't mean it that way. I think reluctance to admit a mistake is human nature, not deliberate dishonesty. Sometimes we can't even admit to ourselves that we were wrong.

"I'd say ninety percent of the brokers I've known are professional and honest.

"The press is constantly alleging that brokers *churn* accounts, meaning they trade them excessively to generate commissions. I saw very little of that while I was a broker. For the most part, I don't think that brokers' poor investment performance has anything to do with ethics. Picking stocks successfully is very difficult, and most of us just aren't capable of doing it. It's as simple as that. And like I said earlier, brokers are salespeople, not investment advisers. The bottom line is, if brokers were really so smart, they wouldn't need clients."

"So we should never use a broker," Tom summarized.

"We didn't say that," Roy clarified. "We said you shouldn't invest your ten percent fund in common stocks on your own or with help from a broker. But there are a lot of fine brokers out there, and used properly, they can be a big help in achieving financial success."

"But what else does a broker do?" I questioned.

"I'll get to one of the ways a broker can help in a minute. In the meantime, let's look at how to invest that ten percent," Roy answered patiently.

"You want us to invest in ownership but not in common stocks. I guess that leaves real estate. What should we do? Buy a square foot each month with our $200?"

Obviously, Tom was kidding, but I thought he had

asked a fairly good question. Is there such a thing as a $200 parcel of land?

"Real estate is a very real possibility," Roy affirmed. "Not by buying a square foot a month, mind you. We'll get into that later, too. First, let's look at what I think is the best alternative for investing the ten percent, at least for people able to leave their money alone for several years — mutual funds."

I frowned. "I thought the stock market was a losing game. Don't mutual funds own primarily common stock?"

"I've read some bad things about mutual funds lately," Cathy added in a worried tone. "A lot of people lost big money in mutuals during the crash, didn't they?"

"I didn't say the stock market is a losing game. I said buying and selling stocks on your own or on your broker's advice is usually a losing game. The stock market has actually been very good to investors who have the qualities we spoke of earlier: intelligence, courage, patience, and an eye for value.

"A carefully selected equity mutual fund gives you access to a professional money manager who has demonstrated those qualities. You won't be making the individual investment decisions. A professional will.

"Simply stated, a mutual fund is a professionally managed pool of money. The pool is made up of money from people like you and me, people numbering in the thousands. We all put our money together and hand it over to someone who knows, or supposedly knows, what he or she's doing. An equity mutual fund owns primarily common stock.

"There are all sorts of benefits. Most important is the one I just mentioned — professional money management. Second, mutuals give you diversification. Most people don't have enough money to buy a properly diversified portfolio, with stocks in different industries in a variety of countries. By pooling resources, individuals can gain a pro-rata share in a vast array of securities. 'Don't put all your eggs in one basket,' and all that stuff. Third, mutual funds are a *hands-off* investment. There is no ongoing research and decision-making process required of the investor. This feature is very important. Most of us don't have time to look after our investments. We work all day. With mutual funds, that isn't a problem. They have a low PITA factor."

"What's a PITA factor?"

"Pain in the Ass factor . . . a highly technical investment term," Roy told us with a chuckle.

"You make mutual funds sound perfect. If they're so great, why do they seem to get a fair amount of bad press?" Cathy challenged.

"Oh, they're far from perfect. Like all equity vehicles — that is, investments involving ownership — they're subject to risk. There are no guarantees, and they do fluctuate up and down. If the market takes a steep fall, your mutual fund will likely tumble with it. If your professional money manager makes a series of bad investment decisions, they'll be reflected in the performance of the fund, no doubt about it.

"And always bear this in mind — if you buy a common-stock fund at the height of the market, you're asking for trouble. 'Buy low, sell high' has long been a cliché of the investment business, but better advice has never been offered. If you rush in and buy a fund, or for that matter any investment, because your neighbour's has tripled in the past five years, you're probably making a mistake. It's when your neighbour's investment has gone down thirty percent over the past two years that you're probably looking at a good time to buy.

"In addition to the fact that it's hard to time your purchase, and that mutual funds are subject to market fluctuations, there are a couple of other drawbacks.

"Equity funds are very long-term investments. Precisely because they're hard to time and they do fluctuate, an investor has to be thinking long term. Over a period of, say, seven to ten years, the economy, and therefore the market, will most likely continue to spiral upward. If you're willing to hold your fund for that length of time, you'll have little to worry about. But if you're buying a fund for a two- or three-year period, you better be a lot smarter than me! I'm confident that the market will perform well over the long run. It always has. But I'm not sure where it's going over the next couple of years. As I've gotten older, I've realized no one else is, either. No one. As for consistently accurate short-term forecasters, there is no such animal.

"One final problem with mutual funds — they're boring. Nobody goes to a party and talks about how their mutual fund went up two cents yesterday. Individual stocks, real estate, options, commodities, these all carry an aura of excitement, a bit of Vegas. Not funds. Nobody's ever called mutual funds an exciting way to invest your money."

"That seems like a lot of problems for what you termed our 'best alternative,'" I pointed out.

"It may seem that way, Dave, but when you examine it closely, it isn't that way at all. I'll prove it one 'problem' at a time.

"First, market fluctuations. Like a roller coasters, they're fun on the way up and scary on the way down. But thanks to the power of *dollar cost averaging*, even downside fluctuations can work to your advantage.

"Dollar cost averaging is as close to infallible investing as you can get. It genuinely slants the odds in an investor's favour, yet I've read all kinds of financial planning books that haven't even mentioned it. Most people haven't even heard of it."

"I haven't," Cathy admitted. "Is it hard to do?"

"It's as easy as pie," Roy assured her. "The technical definition is 'A system of buying common stocks or mutual fund shares at regular intervals with a fixed dollar amount.' Whoop-de-do, eh?

"Let's see how something that sounds so theoretical can easily produce fantastic results.

"Tom, say you decide to save $100 a month and invest it in fund XYZ. The month you start your program, XYZ is trading at ten dollars a share, so obviously you buy ten shares. The second month XYZ has dropped by fifty percent, all the way to five dollars . . . not good. Your $100 now buys you twenty shares. In month three, the fund has rebounded somewhat and now trades at seven dollars and fifty cents, still well under your original purchase price. You buy thirteen and a third shares. So what's happened?"

"I've lost money following your advice. That's what happened," answered Tom.

"No, you haven't," I interrupted confidently. "You've broken even. You're down two-fifty a share on your purchase at ten, you're up two-fifty a share on your purchase at five, and you're even on your final purchase."

Roy corrected us, "You're both wrong."

"I hate math," I growled. "But how can I be wrong? It's just a question of average price. Even I can figure out the average of three numbers."

"How many shares does Tom own?" asked Roy. He then quickly answered his own question: "Forty-three and a third. And how much are the shares currently worth? Seven dollars and fifty cents each. What's forty-three and a third times seven-fifty? Three hundred and twenty-five. How much had Tom invested? Three hundred. He's up twenty-five dollars, an excellent return over such a short period of time."

"How the — "

"Because you're putting in a fixed amount each

month, you obtain more shares at the lower prices. You bought twenty shares at five, but only ten at ten. Basically, it means that your average cost per share will be lower than the average price per share. In the long run, or even in the short run, that bodes well for the investor.

"So one month when the stock market is struggling and your mutual fund is suffering accordingly, don't look at the situation and say, 'Darn, my holding is down.' Look at it and say, 'Eventually the market will go up and take the value of my holding with it, so in the meantime I'm going to pick up shares at a good price.' Dollar cost averaging is great stuff!

"With mutuals, problem number two is timing. It's very difficult for an amateur, or even a professional, to time a purchase accurately. Well, it's no problem at all when you buy monthly. We're not buying once; we're buying continuously. Sometimes we'll buy high, but sometimes we'll buy low. When the market goes into a prolonged slump, there we are, picking up shares at good prices, month after month. Forget discipline, courage, intelligence, and an eye for value. We don't need any of them. We buy every month.

"Does Black Monday hurt our holdings? Sure it does. But the market will bounce back. It always does. And while it's down, we're picking shares up at rock-bottom prices and a lot of shares, thanks to dollar cost averaging."

"I guess the fact that mutual funds are long-term investments isn't a problem, either," Cathy mused. "We're going to be accumulating and holding shares for ten, twenty, maybe even thirty years. We are the consummate long-term investors. As you said, short-term downturns, even prolonged downturns, will work to our advantage, not to our detriment. This sounds great, Roy!"

"It is great, Cathy. And as far as mutual funds not

being a glamorous investment, well, so what? After they've earned you good returns, you can use the profits to buy more exciting things if you want . . . such as the satellite dish I bought yesterday."

"Get out! Dave and I will be over tomorrow to watch the Tigers' game. Put a few on ice, will you, Roy?"

"I love you guys like sons, but if you ever come near my house, I'll call the police."

"Some father you must be," Tom grumbled.

An intrigued Cathy pressed on. "What mutual funds should we buy, Roy, and how do we purchase them?"

"Good questions. I'm going to leave it to the three of you to select your own funds, but let me give you a few pointers.

"Too often, mutual funds are discussed in blanket terms. 'I don't like mutual funds.' 'I heard about someone who made a killing in mutual funds.' That type of thing. But all mutual funds are not created equal. Some I like; some I don't.

"The key is the manager. You're buying professional money management, and there can be as big a difference between two professional money managers as there can be between two professional hockey players. If I asked you, 'Who do you want on your team, Dave Semenko or Wayne Gretzky?' I feel certain you'd all answer the Great One. When you're selecting a fund, find the Gretzky of money management."

"How do we do that?"

"If you were assigned to select the best player in the NHL but didn't follow hockey, where would you start? You'd look at statistics, of course. Who is the highest point-getter? Who's the most consistent? Has he been good for just one year, or has he proven he can do it year after year? When times are tough and his team is struggling, does he maintain a high level of play or drop off badly? Once you had studied the statistics, you would read some articles and talk to people in the know. What are the experts' opinions? Do they jibe with your findings?

"It's no different when you're looking for a good mutual fund. Assess past records. They don't guarantee future results, but they sure as heck are a good indication of the manager's abilities. What's the five-year average return? Ten-year? Fifteen-year? Does the fund perform consistently or is it way up one year and way down the next? How does it fare during the bad times? Some funds have excellent records during tough times.

"Then talk to the experts. Go see a stockbroker, a mutual fund salesperson, or a life insurance salesperson. What do they think? Read a few investment publications. The *Financial Times* and the *Financial Post* do tremendous jobs monitoring mutual fund performance and highlighting industry leaders. In fact, once a month both of these fine periodicals have in-depth mutual fund summary charts that include performance figures for various lengths of time, variability rates, commission charges, and pretty much everything else you could possibly want to know."

"Can't you give us any other tips, Roy?" Cathy pleaded. "We need all the help we can get!"

"For you, anything. Okay. Point one: make sure that if a fund has solid rates of return, the manager who created them is still there. You're not buying past performance numbers; you're buying a manager's expertise. If fund ABC averaged twenty percent a year under the guidance of Jack Smith, but Jack Smith has left, stay away from ABC. You can't be sure what you're getting.

"Two: buy an international fund that invests across many different industries. You don't want to buy a fund that only invests in one country or one industry; that's poor diversification. Specialty funds, as they're known, are much riskier investments than international funds.

"Three: buy a fund whose manager is value oriented. By that I mean someone who doesn't chase fads or try to be wherever the action is. Find someone who uses common sense, discipline, and patience to select and hold stocks that offer good value, stocks that at the time of purchase others are overlooking. A broker or fund salesperson will be able to help you out here.

"Four: watch your commissions. The fund I used had a high commission structure, but it was well worth the cost. Nonetheless, it's certainly in your best interest to limit your front-end load. That load is often as high as nine percent, so for every dollar you put in, nine cents comes right off the top. There are some good no-load funds. If you can't find one you like, remember the vast majority of load funds have fully negotiable commissions. However, the commissions should be the last factor you look at when deciding what fund to buy, and if the mutual fund salesperson you're dealing with offers good advice and solid service, a high front-end load may well be worth it.

"Five: many financial product salespeople are confined to selling only their companies' own products. This isn't necessarily bad, as many of those products are quite acceptable, but these salespeople's natural bias is something to keep in mind when weighing their advice.

"Finally, I want to reemphasize the importance of a good long-term track record. Anybody can get hot for a few years, but if someone has had superior rates of return for a fifteen- or twenty-year period, that's a good indication that he knows what he's doing . . . Oops, sorry, Cathy.

"As for how to buy a fund on a monthly plan, it's as easy as signing your name. All you have to do is fill out a preauthorized chequing plan and a fund-purchase application. They're often on the same form. It won't take you more than a minute. Oh, and don't ever sign contractual plans. They limit your freedom. If the fund manager left and you wanted to switch funds, a contractual plan would restrict your flexibility through penalty clauses. Just stick to a PAC plan, a preauthorized chequing plan, that you can cancel anytime.

"Each month, the fund will forward you a summary of your current situation: how much you contributed this month; how many shares that money bought and at what price; your accumulated share position — everything. These statements explain it all. You just stick them in your file and watch the money grow, all the while thinking what a great guy your barber is."

"Do they mail you the shares each month?"

"No. For convenience' sake, the shares are kept in noncertificate form at the mutual fund company. But if you ever want a share certificate, it's only a letter away."

"What if you want to cash out and get your money?"

"That's only a letter away, too. But you won't be doing that for a long, long time, will you, Tom?"

"Of course not, Roy. I was just curious."

I cut in. "What about taxes, Roy? Do you pay them each year?"

"That's another beauty of equity mutual funds compared to plain old money in the bank. Not only do you reap the benefits of dollar cost averaging and the higher rates of return over the long run created through ownership, but you also pay a lower tax rate on your gains.

"Interest is fully taxable. However, currently each of you can earn up to $100,000 of captial gains —

growth, that is — through your equity funds tax-free. And after you've taken advantage of that great tax break, only three-quarters of the rest of your gains are taxable. What's more, you don't pay any capital-gains tax until you sell, so all your money works for you full-time! Occasionally, the fund might pay a small interest dividend that is fully taxable, but with a growth fund, the type you're buying, it will be a very small amount.

"Speaking of dividends," our wealthy barber continued, "that's another thing I should explain. Mutual funds make money in three ways. Most of a growth fund's profit occurs when the fund sells stock for more than it paid for it — in other words, a capital gain. A fund also makes money when one of the stocks it owns pays it a dividend. Finally, a fund earns interest income from bonds and idle cash. At least once a year, the fund declares dividends to distribute the profits from all three of these sources. It's extremely important that at the time of purchase you instruct the fund management to reinvest your dividends in the form of additional shares. That's when the compounding effect really kicks in.

"One final point before we leave mutual funds. Another major reason mutual funds are preferable to just leaving your money in the bank is that they're less accessible. Very few of us have the willpower to resist the temptation that a growing bank account poses. As a result, a lot of people dip into their savings. Redeeming funds requires writing a letter, having your signature guaranteed, and registering your letter before mailing, giving us the time to think twice. These little nuisances help discourage human impulsiveness, if you will."

"You said mutual funds are probably our number-one choice for investing the ten percent. What are the others?"

"Dave, my boy, there are literally hundreds of options. You could buy gold, Chinese ceramics, stamps, whatever. But for obvious reasons, those are not good choices. Certainly, mutual funds are almost perfect for our monthly savings — "

"That is, a well-selected mutual fund," I interrupted.

"That is, a well-selected mutual fund," Roy confirmed amiably. "But there is one other viable alternative. Surprisingly, it's the one Tom joked about earlier — real estate."

"How do you buy real estate for $200 a month?" Cathy and Tom chimed in in stereo.

"Alas, with only $200 a month it is impossible, but with $400 or $500, it may be possible.

"Let's say you took out a personal loan right now at around thirteen percent. If you borrowed $20,000 and amortized the loan, paid it back in full, in other words, over five years, it would cost you about $450 a month.

"But let's say instead of using the $20,000 to buy a car, you used it as a down payment on an $80,000 condominium. Your mortgage would obviously be for $60,000. You then rent the condo out for $600 a month plus utilities and upkeep.

"The end result is that your rent covers your mortgage. Your expenses are covered by your tenant. Your only cost is your monthly loan payment of $450.

"Five years later, you sell the condo for $130,000, a very realistic figure representing an average annual compound return of just over ten percent. Your personal loan of $20,000 is no longer around . . . you've paid it off. The outstanding principal on your mortgage is about $57,000, as most of your $600 monthly payment has been applied to the interest on the mortgage. One hundred and thirty minus fifty-seven is seventy-three. You're left with $73,000, less your tax liability, that is."

"Four hundred and fifty bucks a month for five years parlayed into $73,000. C'mon. It's too easy," Tom said in disbelief.

"Not only that," James Murray added, "but there can be some tax advantages to using borrowed money to buy real estate."

"Then why isn't every man, woman, and child doing it?" I asked.

"You'd be surprised how many people are doing it, or something similar to it. It's said that ninety per-cent of the world's millionaires have become million-aires through real estate. Mind you, it isn't as easy as it sounds. There are potential problems.

"The main one is, what happens if the property value declines instead of rising? People out in Calgary who bought in the early eighties are still trying to recover. In many cases, their proceeds from a property sale didn't even cover the mortgage balance. They had negative savings! That's a frightening concept.

"With real estate, it's a matter of timing. There's no dollar cost averaging here. No safety net. So you'd better be right when you buy that property. The one big thing investors do have in their favour, though, is real estate's phenomenal record of rising prices. It seldom collapses. In fact, in some locales, it rarely falls at all, but . . . but . . . " Roy wagged his finger.

"The only thing worse than a bad investment is a bad investment made with borrowed money. Dave, can you see yourself telling your wife that you just lost $20,000, twenty thousand borrowed dollars?"

"She'd kill me." I gulped, knowing the prediction was accurate.

"Kill yourself first," Tom suggested helpfully.

"The timing of the purchase isn't the only problem. Interest rates can turn against you, too. Sure, they're down now, but what if five years down the road, when your mortgage comes due, they're back up at eigh-teen? Then all of a sudden your mortgage payment skyrockets to $870, and because of rent control, you can't get the rent increase you need from your tenant. The heartbreak of negative cash flow results. Say this happens at a time when your business is suffering, too, Cathy. What do you do?"

"Sell."

"Sounds good, but with rates that high, very few people can afford to buy. Demand is way down, and a lot of people are trying to sell. You're not the only one hurt by the higher financing costs! End result — your property value is down. If you have no choice but to sell, you'll have to sell at a loss," he ended ominously.

"Roy, you're scaring them off the finest investment a person could make!" James Murray complained. "I mean, really, how many people do you know who have lost money in real estate?"

"I just want the kids to be aware there are risks."

"That's fine, but — "

"Hold on, hold on. Let me finish. The other problem with real estate is that it has a very high PITA factor. Finding tenants, fixing toilets at two in the morning, mowing lawns . . . It's a lot of work. Some people thrive on that stuff. They're great with their hands and real estate provides them with a profitable way to enjoy their hobby. But if you're not that type of person, beware."

"The only thing I've fixed in my life is my cat," Tom kibitzed.

Jimmy and Clyde loved that one.

"So I gather you're endorsing the fund route?" By now, my sister was on the edge of her seat.

"Initially, yes. In your early years of saving ten percent, I think the funds are a better way to go. You're busy starting your careers, raising families, buying homes, and all that. Real estate takes a lot of time. Also, the funds make more sense from a diversification standpoint, in that you'll probably own your own homes soon, so you'll already have some real estate.

"Besides, most people in their twenties, thirties, and early forties aren't in good enough financial shape to qualify for a down-payment loan, anyway — unless, of course, they borrow it privately or have a cosigner. And even then, most institutions and lending regulations frown on borrowed down payments. Plus, the $100,000 capital-gains exemption is no longer available for real estate — that hurts.

"What I did, and what I think you should do, is buy mutual funds with the ten percent for several years. When I had built up a good nest egg, I switched to real estate. Forgive the pun, but you don't want all your nest eggs in one basket. Plus, because I had a nest egg, I knew that if interest rates rose or real estate prices dropped, I wouldn't be forced to sell. I had the luxury of being able to be patient. Patience is always one of the most valuable attributes in investing, and nowhere is that more true than in real estate. It may go down, but it seldom stays there.

"I've kept you three a long time today. Longer than I had planned." By the time Roy said this, Tom and I had long since had our haircuts finished. In fact, Tom needed a trim already. James Murray's grey hair was now joining our locks on the floor.

"I want to tell you a quick story before I let you go," Roy decided. "But before I do, are there any questions?"

"Should we buy more than one fund?"

"Well, Cathy, a fund by its very nature offers solid diversification, so I really don't think it's necessary, although it probably wouldn't hurt. In fact, to take advantage of different management approaches, yeah, it might be good to invest in two or three funds — but I never did."

"You talked a lot about selecting a mutual fund, but what about selecting a property?" I inquired.

"Talk to a professional. We're in the presence of

greatness right here," he indicated, acknowledging James Murray. "In Kitchener, Dave, you'll have to locate someone with a good reputation. It shouldn't be hard. Ask around. In addition, there's a plethora of good real estate books available at the library that talk about everything from selecting a good location to the tax implications of owning a property. No questions, Tom?"

"Just one. What's a *plethora*?"

"I have another question," I stated above the laughter. "What about RRSPs and paying down the mortgage? Aren't those supposed to be smart things to do? Wouldn't they be wise investments for the ten percent?"

"Those are excellent investments, and we'll talk about both of them in the upcoming months. But the ten-percent saving is different. It's separate. It's our I've-made-it-big fund, and it's intended to give us the finer things in life. The things we dream of one day owning and couldn't afford otherwise — a Mercedes, a winter home, early retirement or in Tom's case . . . a girlfriend.

"And the beauty of it is, it's not hard to do. The so-called sacrifice is barely noticeable. By saving ten percent of your pay now, you virtually guarantee yourself financial freedom later in life. Only a fool would say no to that. So start now, and don't stop!"

"In the words of Syrus, 'Many receive advice; only the wise profit from it,'" James Murray elaborated. "Just thinking about saving ten percent has never made anyone wealthy."

"Like I said, I have just the story to convince you before you go," Roy remembered. "It will be of particular interest to you, Dave, because the individual involved is a teacher, too.

"Three or four years ago, a fellow came in. He explained that he wasn't here simply for a haircut, but also because he had heard that I'm a financial planning expert. He was wondering if he could send his twenty-two-year-old son to me to learn the basics. 'I don't know a thing about insurance, stocks, real estate or any of that stuff,' he confessed. 'The only thing I know about financial planning is to save ten percent of all you make and invest it for long-term growth. The rest of it's Greek to me.'

"Well, it turns out this man's father had been a friend of old Mr. White's and he, too, had been fortunate enough to have learned the golden secret. He passed it along to his young son, but unlike me, this teacher hadn't furthered his knowledge of financial planning. As he said, he knew nothing about insurance and investing. What's worse, I learned through our conversation that he had abused credit cards over the years, not started an RRSP, and had lost all $15,000 of an inheritance playing the commodities market."

"This is a real upbeat story, Roy. Very encouraging," Tom drawled, tongue in cheek.

"At the time of our meeting, that teacher's net worth was almost $650,000, Tom. Some of it, maybe $150,000, represented his home and personal belongings. The rest of it had been created from his ten-percent fund. What's more, his wife had only chosen to work for four years."

"He did everything else wrong but   " Cathy began.

"Because he had saved ten percent of each pay cheque and invested it for long-term growth, today he's in great shape," Roy finished.

He then walked purposefully over to the counter. A second later, we heard two clicks. Roy then turned and handed my sister a cassette tape of our entire conversation.

"I thought this might come in handy for those who don't take shorthand," he commiserated, looking pointedly at me.

"Good," I said with a laugh. "It will save Cathy having to transcribe her notes for us. Well, Roy, what does next month's *adventure in accumulating* hold in store for us?"

"For now, why don't you three just worry about implementing this month's suggestions?" Roy responded.

"It's inspiring to know how wealthy Roy is," Tom joked within earshot of Roy as we walked back out into the downpour. "But don't you think we're insulting him by offering to pay for our haircuts?"

"You boys," came Roy's rejoinder, "are all wet."

5
WILLS, LIFE
INSURANCE, AND
RESPONSIBILITY

"Well, well," Roy greeted us as we came in from the sunshine. "Has it been a month already? It seems as though you three were here just last week."

"They say time flies at your age, Roy," Tom teased.

"Cathy, you look gorgeous, as always. Tom, you don't. Hey, Dave, when's school out? Your vacation must start soon."

"Week after next. Sue and I will stick around Kitchener until mid-July, and then we'll be here for five fun-filled weeks at the cottage we've rented in Bright's Grove. You should drop by for a barbecue one night, Roy . . . but don't tell Clyde," I added loudly enough for Clyde to hear. He just smirked and doffed his Blue Jays baseball cap.

"Roy, you're going to be really proud of us," Cathy began, always one to turn a conversation serious. "All three of us have started our save-ten-percent programs."

"That's great! Did you use preauthorized chequing to buy mutual funds?" Roy asked.

"Cathy and I did," I answered. "Tom went another route. But before he tells you about it, I've got a quick story for you. I was passing on what you taught us to some teachers in the staff room. They couldn't believe those compound interest examples. Even the math teachers were amazed! I explained why a monthly purchase plan of mutual funds was such a good idea — dollar cost averaging, forced saving, long-term growth . . . even the low PITA factor. Everything. Most of the teachers seemed really interested, but a couple were skeptical. Then Mary McGrath, our English department head, spoke up. She said that fifteen years ago she had started a preauthorized chequing plan to purchase a well-known growth fund, with $500 up front and $100 a month. She has had all her dividends reinvested and has never withdrawn a cent. Today, her fund is worth almost $85,000 . . . and that's with only $100 over a mere fifteen years! I'll tell you, that impressed them! When one of the teachers in his mid-forties asked if it was too late for him, Mary replied, 'The best time to plant an oak tree was twenty years ago. The second best time is now.' Great line, huh?"

"I couldn't have said it better myself." Roy nodded approvingly. "Obviously, starting young will benefit you tremendously, but so will starting today. Oh, sure, you won't save as much starting later, but even a forty-five-year-old can still save a significant sum — very significant. As you pointed out, look what your teacher friend has accomplished in only fifteen years with a fairly small monthly saving."

"I was in my mid-forties when I started paying myself first, and I've done real good," Clyde contributed.

"I've done really well," I corrected him.

"You too, Dave? That's great" was his quick comeback.

"So, Tom, what's this other route?" Roy inquired slowly, probably still stunned by Clyde's unusual display of wit.

"Well, Roy, I know that you recommend mutual

funds over real estate in the early years, but I had an opportunity I couldn't turn down.

"I told my brother what you taught us last month and he was really pumped up. He suggested that he and I go together to buy a property. The place beside his had been for sale for a couple of months. It's small and needs a lot of work, but it has definite possibilities. Brian said that if we bought it together, he would do all the yard work and all the repairs and renovations. My job would be to find a reliable tenant and handle the paperwork. We had James come out and take a look, and he agreed that with the proximity to the water, the size of the lot, and the good neighbourhood, the property was definitely underpriced. The deal closes next month.

"We're borrowing $24,000 and amortizing the loan over five years. That's going to cost us $270 a month each. We're putting $20,000 down and using the other $4,000 to fix the place up a bit. Our mortgage is for $57,000. Principal, interest, and taxes are going to cost us about $670 a month."

"Have you found a tenant?" Roy asked.

"That's the beautiful part, Roy," Tom answered eagerly. "Kyle MacKenzie and his wife have signed a three-year lease with us for $680 a month, plus utilities."

"It really is a sweet deal, Roy," James Murray broke in. "In five years I wouldn't be surprised if the place was worth $140,000. They've got a good tenant, balanced cash flow, low interest-rate exposure, and Tom All-Thumbs here doesn't even have to get his hands dirty."

"I'm impressed, Tom. 'You done good,' as Clyde would say. I still think that for most young people mutual funds are the best alternative, but you're a good example of why the word always is a dangerous one."

"Thanks, Roy. It's funny, but on the way here, all

three of us agreed that even though it's only been one month, we feel a lot better about our finances already. For the first time in my life, I actually believe I will be wealthy someday. It's great."

"Yeah, Roy, and you know what else?" Cathy beamed. "Like Tom said, it's only been a month, but I haven't missed that ten percent at all, just like you promised."

"Don't get a big head, Roy. Your advice last month may have been great, but I'm not all that happy with my haircut," I kidded.

"I guess I'll have to get a new bowl," Roy quipped. "Are you three ready for the second lesson? I'd better warn you, it's not quite as exciting — "

"Or as long, I hope," Tom interjected.

"Or as long," Roy confirmed. "But in a different way, today is just as important. We're going to look at estate planning. You know . . . wills, life insurance . . . those fun things."

"And to think that I looked forward to this for a month," Cathy groaned.

"Maybe wills and insurance aren't the most thrilling topics in the world, but they sure are important. More people foul up in this area than any other part of financial planning.

"More than half the people I know don't even have a will. That's ridiculous. And as for life insurance . . . well, most Canadians have the wrong kind, the wrong amount, and often even have the wrong person insured."

"Yeah. I read an article the other day saying that Canadians are overinsured," I pointed out, thinking that for once I'd look informed.

"Wrong," replied Roy. "Dead wrong. Being one of the most insured countries on a per capita basis and being overinsured are not synonymous. Canadians, for the most part, are not overinsured. Some obviously are, but the majority of us are underinsured . . . in some cases, dramatically . . . even alarmingly so.

"But we'll talk more about insurance in a few minutes. First I want to deal with wills.

"You know estate planning is really nothing more than what you do before you die to make sure that the people and things that you care about are well taken care of after your death. You want your *living estate* — in other words, your assets less your liabilities — combined with your insurance proceeds, to provide the necessary capital to carry out your wishes. Your will should make sure that that capital is distributed according to your wishes.

"The importance of an up-to-date will cannot be overstated. Contrary to what most people believe, if you die without a will, things will not automatically work out as you would have wished. Disaster can result.

"Dave, let's say your father were to die tomorrow. If he didn't have a will, what do you think would happen?"

"My mother would inherit everything?" I hazarded, shrugging my shoulders.

"No. I'll bet the court decides. They'll look at how many children there are, how old they are, and all that stuff," Cathy ventured in a somewhat more confident tone.

"You're both wrong," stated Roy. "When no will is available, the estate assets are frozen and the court winds up the deceased's affairs and pays off his or her debts. The remaining estate is then divided according to a rigid set of rules found in the provincial intestacy laws."

"Intestacy?" Cathy and Tom echoed in chorus.

"*Intestacy*, from *intestate* . . . having made no will," Roy explained.

"No thought is given to the deceased's known wishes or to the needs of the potential inheritors. For example, even if a surviving spouse needed a great deal of money for medical reasons, the estate would still be allotted according to the rules. The bulk of the estate might be tied up in a government-administered trust until the children reached the age of majority.

"If your father died, the first $75,000 would go to your mother. The remainder of the estate would be divided, one-third for your mother, two-thirds for you two kids."

"So in our case, the remainder would be one-third each," I summarized.

"Exactly, although the Family Law Act may come into play.

"Regardless, I think you'll agree with me that it's your dad's wish for your mom to have everything and then, on her death, for you children to inherit the family estate. Who knows? Over the years she may need the entire amount."

"Boy, you two had better hope your dad doesn't have a will," Jimmy wisecracked.

"Charitable donations, scholarship awards, gifts for grandchildren or godchildren . . . none of these will be taken care of if there is no will.

"Even if you're single, you should have a will. Cathy, if you died tomorrow, your entire estate would go to your parents. That may be what you want, but more than likely it isn't," Roy continued.

"You're right, Roy, it isn't. I'd like to leave Dave and Sue something. I mean, they need it more than Mom and Dad do. And I'd like to leave the Big Sister organization something for all the fine work they do. And Dave and Sue have asked me to be godmother to their baby. I never thought about it before, but I really do need a will."

"Me too," I added. "When I die, I want to make sure everything goes to Sue and doesn't get tied up in a trust for years. That's no good."

"Even I need a will," mused Tom. "I'm not really all

that close to my dad, and even if I was, he certainly doesn't need the money as much as my brother and sister do."

"Don't forget your best friend, either," I reminded him.

"All right. I don't think it's necessary to go around the room stating why each of us needs a will or you'll end up being here longer than you were last month. The point is that everyone does need a will, period. We haven't even talked about problems that intestacy can cause for common-law spouses and business partners. It gets pretty scary."

"How do you make a will?" wondered Cathy.

"First, don't do it yourself. Go to a professional. Most lawyers have experience in drawing up wills and in estate planning.

"Second, before you go to a lawyer, sit down and map out exactly what your estate would consist of and how you want it to be divided. If you're married, make sure your spouse sits down with you.

"Third, choose an executor. This is the person or trust company that will carry out your will's instructions. The executor has to do everything from making the funeral arrangements to notifying the beneficiaries to applying for Canada Pension Plan benefits to filing an income tax return and a lot more. It's a heavy responsibility.

"So if you choose an individual as an executor, make sure he or she lives near you. It's unfair to ask your cousin Eddy to fly across the country to wind up your affairs, especially since it may involve several trips. Also, choose someone your age or younger. It doesn't make sense to name your father or aunt as executor when the odds are they'll predecease you. And don't be too quick to name your spouse! If he or she has no money management skills, there may be other more suitable choices. Besides, your spouse is going to have a hard enough time without having to handle all the work involved in being an executor. Coexecutors are a good alternative. Your spouse and a friend with a business background would be perfect. Two final points about choosing an executor: one: for obvious reasons, choose someone who is absolutely honest and reliable; two: don't forget to name contingent executors in case your first choice is unwilling or unable to act when the time comes."

"Boy, you sure were right, Roy," Tom commented.

"About the importance of a will?"

"No. About this not being as exciting as last month."

"Ha, ha! Actually, you'll find the part on insurance very interesting. Just let me wrap up wills.

"A fourth thing to keep in mind is that large potential capital-gains taxes, business ownership, divorces, alimony, remarriages, et cetera, et cetera can all complicate the estate-planning process. Make sure the lawyer you're using is fully aware of any potential problem areas. Lawyers know how to plan for all the standard problems, like the simultaneous death of two spouses, but they're not mind readers. They can't know all the relevant details of your personal situation unless you tell them.

"The fifth and last point to keep in mind is that you must keep your will updated. Births, deaths, divorces, business deals, whatever may make a will obsolete. Review your will at least once a year, and for heaven's sake, make sure that your executors know where to find it! In fact, give them a copy and keep another copy at your lawyer's.

"Oh, and always keep a complete, up-to-date net-worth statement, listing everything you own and everything you owe, along with a copy of your will, in your safe-deposit box. A friend of mine died ten years ago and they didn't discover until last year that he owned shares in a number of large companies.

The certificates were registered in the brokerage company's name and held on account, and the firm had never been notified of his death. A lawyer I know tells me this kind of thing happens frequently."

"How much does it cost to draw up a will?" I inquired.

"A straightforward will, the kind most of us need, costs about $100. In view of its importance, that's certainly not a lot of money to spend."

"I don't know why, but I always figured a will would cost a lot more than that."

"No. It's not the cost of a will that prevents most Canadians from having one. It's just pure procrastination. We all know we're going to die someday, but we don't want to admit that day could be soon, so we put off planning for it. But you three won't do that. Do you know how I can be so sure?"

"Because you know we're responsible people?" Tom speculated.

"No. Because next month each of you is going to bring me a copy of your lawyer's bill showing that you've had a will drawn up. If you don't, the fountain of your financial knowledge will suddenly dry up."

"Roy," Cathy protested, "we're not little kids. We're mature adults."

"Speak for yourself!" Tom roared.

"We all started our save-ten-percent program without being forced to, didn't we?" my sister persevered.

"Good point, Cathy. Very good point. But bring me the bill, anyway," Roy commanded, over the chuckles of James Murray.

Procrastination is my middle name, but I didn't need Roy's strong-arm tactics to get me moving. After learning about intestacy laws, I decided that only a fool wouldn't have a will. One hundred dollars is an insignificant price to pay when you consider what's at stake.

"The bottom line is, Roy, that if you don't have a will, your loved ones could suffer," I concluded aloud. "I'm not going to do that to my survivors."

"Well said, Dave. But bring me the bill next month, anyway."

"Roy did the same thing with me," Clyde piped up. "Treated me just like a kid. You know what I did to get him back? I bequeathed him my little dog."

"I can't believe that," James Murray scoffed.

"It's true. You can ask Roy."

"No, no. Not the part about the dog. What I can't believe is you knowing the word *bequeath*!"

"Just be sure Mrs. Murray wears a name tag to my funeral, James," Clyde warned him. "I worry that Roy might accidentally take her home with him and leave my dog alone back in my apartment."

"I hate to break up this scintillating dialogue, but we've got more material to cover." Roy's announcement immediately silenced Sarnia's Laurel and Hardy.

"On to insurance. Let me caution you now to pay strict attention to the rest of today's lesson. I say this for four reasons: one: the financial future of your loved ones may depend on you having the proper amount of life insurance; two: it is without a doubt essential to your own financial future that you have the right type of life insurance; three: there's a good chance that James and I are the only two people you'll ever meet who have a full understanding of insurance and who are willing to share that understanding with you, and four: my tape recorder is broken."

"What about insurance agents?" Cathy asked.

"Are you kid — "

"Whoa, slow down, James. Slow down," interrupted Roy. "We'll talk more about insurance agents in a few minutes. For now, suffice it to say that there are some good insurance agents and some who are not so good."

"Many who are not so good," James Murray grumbled.

"Perhaps," Roy agreed. "But that holds true in any occupation. There are good teachers and bad teachers, good real estate agents and bad real estate agents — "

"Good-looking wives and bad-looking wives," Clyde shot at James.

"The problem with insurance is that most people are so poorly informed that they have no way of telling the good agent from the bad agent. If I consistently give you a bad haircut, you'll eventually stop coming here."

"Gee, we haven't yet," I remarked.

"Cute, Dave. But with an insurance agent's advice, it's different. It's intangible. Its worth can only be measured by an informed observer. So the answer is simple; become an informed observer! Fortunately, that's not as difficult as you might think.

"Let's get started. Cathy, why do people buy life insurance?" Roy asked.

"Well, uh, what do you mean?" she stammered, surprised to be singled out.

"Just what I said. Why do people buy life insurance?"

"Well, if you die prematurely, you want to have enough money to support your spouse and kids, I guess."

"Close. People buy, strike that, *should* buy life insurance so that when they die, their living estate — again, that's their assets less their liabilities — combined with their insurance proceeds, can allow for the proper winding down of their financial affairs and provide the desired standard of living for their dependants. Now that's pretty basic, isn't it?"

A collective "Yes" was offered.

"Fine." Roy nodded as he turned back toward Cathy. "Bearing that in mind, how much insurance do you need, Cathy?"

"I just bought a $50,000 policy."

"I didn't ask how much you have. I asked how much you need," Roy reminded her politely.

"Apparently not $50,000." Cathy frowned. "I don't know . . . I guess . . . " She paused to think.

"How much would your dependants need?" Roy asked.

"I don't have any dependants," my puzzled sister responded.

Roy nodded his head slowly and emphatically.

"None. You're saying I don't need any life insurance?"

"That's precisely what I'm saying. Life insurance is a wonderful thing. It's no doubt the most important of all financial arrangements. It is a must until a sufficient living estate has been acquired to protect one's dependants. Purchased properly, it provides people with a relatively inexpensive way to guarantee their dependants a targeted standard of living if premature death occurs. Really, life insurance is better termed *financial protection for dependants*, or *income replacement insurance*. But despite all that, you have to remember it's still an expense. The life insurance companies aren't giving it away. So, like everything else that costs money, it should be bought only when you have a need for it.

"Think about car insurance for a moment. It's wonderful, too. But no one in his right mind would buy it if he didn't own a car. Well, buying life insurance when you have no need for it is equally foolish."

"Shouldn't I at least have enough insurance to cover my funeral expenses?" Cathy wondered.

"In addition to taking care of your dependants, your living estate and your insurance proceeds combined must also allow for the proper winding down of your financial affairs. That includes eliminating all debts, settling taxes, treating business partners and employees fairly, and paying funeral expenses. If your living estate is sufficient to do that, no insurance is needed. For most single people, that's the case," Roy replied.

"Hmm . . . " Cathy started slowly. "My assets would definitely cover my debts and my funeral costs with money left over."

"Mine too," Tom realized. "As of right now, I don't have any debts and the $25,000 group insurance coverage I get as a benefit at work should cover my funeral."

"Twenty-five thousand! That's a heck of a funeral," Clyde said, whistling. "I'll look forward to it, Tom."

"Theoretically, this sounds fine, Roy, but I have a few questions," Cathy persisted. "When I bought my policy last week, the agent insisted it was the smart thing to do for a number of reasons. Some of those reasons still seem to make sense, even though I have no dependants. The first is that my policy is also acting as a saving vehicle for my retirement. The second is that insurance is cheaper to buy when you're young. The third is that I should buy insurance now, when I know I can get it. I can't be sure that in five years, when I may need it, I'll still qualify for it."

"Nonsense, nonsense, and nonsense," muttered James Murray, still glaring at Clyde over his coffee.

"Quite frankly, James is right," Roy conceded. "None of those reasons holds water. You'll see that as we continue our lesson. In fact, if you pay close attention, you'll be able to explain yourself why each of those reasons for buying is 'nonsense.'

"Right now, though, I want to concentrate on how to analyze your insurance needs properly. Tom, how much insurance do I need?"

"Zero. Your living estate, as you put it, is sufficient to provide for your wife and kids. You are, after all, the wealthy barber," Tom answered confidently.

"By George, I think he's got it!" Roy turned to me. "Dave, how much insurance should you buy on your baby's life?"

"Zero. No one is dependent on the baby," I replied with equal confidence.

"Very good," our instructor said approvingly. "Although we love them dearly, children are financial liabilities, not assets. You don't insure a liability! If you had an uncle move in with you, eat your food, drink your beer, and watch TV all day, would you insure him? Of course not! He's a liability. Although parents would cringe at that comparison, I hope you three get the point.

"You only buy insurance when there is a definite need to protect your dependants and to help in winding down your financial affairs. Single people, therefore, often don't need insurance. Young married couples, especially those with children, almost always need insurance. The question for them then becomes not 'Do we need it?' but 'How much do we need?'

"Often the answer to that is, 'More than you think.' Your living estate, not including your noninvestment assets, plus your insurance proceeds must provide enough capital to accomplish a number of things. One: all debt *must* be paid off. The last thing the surviving spouse needs is to be saddled with debt. Two: enough capital must be available to cover future lump-sum obligations. This is something that's often forgotten . . . your funeral expenses, for example. A better example, though, would be college expenses for the children. It costs quite a bit of money to send a child to college or university. Although the child should be responsible for a fair amount of the total cost, he or she may need help. That money to help has to come from somewhere. It should be taken into account when analyzing insurance needs. Three: there must be enough capital and other sources of income present to provide sufficient cash flow to support your dependants. If you feel that your family would need $40,000 a year to live comfortably and their noninvestment income after your death would be only $10,000, your living estate and insurance proceeds would then have to provide a block of capital sufficient to bring in the other $30,000 annually. How much is that? Well, unfortunately, most people arrive at that answer by assuming they will always be able to earn a guaranteed ten percent on their money. That assumption leads them to believe they need a capital pool of $300,000."

"I don't see any problems with that logic," I confessed.

"The problem is that you can't be sure you'll always be able to earn a ten percent rate of return. When it comes to loved ones, you're better to err on the conservative side. I would base my calculations on an eight percent assumed rate of return. So to generate $30,000, I would need a $370,000 pool of capital.

"The last thing your living estate plus insurance proceeds must cover is often totally neglected by people. *Inflation!* Inflation is a widow's or widower's number-one enemy. For example, an insurance program is designed so that a widow is left with an annual income of $35,000, the desired amount. The problem is that the entire $35,000 is needed to support the family; none is saved for the future. Ten years later, that $35,000 may be worth only $15,000 in purchasing-power terms. A middle-aged, untrained woman is forced to go back to work, and even then the family has trouble surviving. Unlikely? Hardly! That's exactly what happened to my wife's aunt . . . and to many, many other people. Inflation's eroding effect on purchasing power is as great as compound interest's growth effect on monthly savings. It must be taken into account. It sometimes means buying up to an additional $100,000 of coverage. But so be it. It must be done.

"Dave, let's look at your case. Pretend that it's a year from now. You've bought your home, and you and Sue are proud parents. How much insurance do you need? And how much insurance should you buy on Sue's life?"

"With our down-payment fund gone towards the purchase of the house, we won't have any investment assets to speak of, so the insurance proceeds are going to have to cover all Sue's and the baby's needs," I responded.

"Good," Roy commended me. "Continue."

"First, we'll have to have a lump sum available to eliminate our debts. I should say debt. The only money that we'll owe will be our mortgage of, say, $80,000.

"Future lump-sum obligations. Hmm . . . Davey, Jr.'s college education, the funeral expenses, and within a couple of years, a new car."

"Fifteen thousand should more than cover the education costs. There will be eighteen years to invest the money and make it grow," Roy explained.

"And $10,000 for burial costs and $15,000 for the car. So future lump-sum obligations total $40,000," I tallied. "Then there's the need for a sufficient income. You know, I don't want Sue to feel she has to work outside the home . . . especially before the baby's in school. So I think I'm going to assume her income after my death will be confined to the $10,000 a year she makes freelancing as a travel writer. To live comfortably, she'll probably need about $30,000 a year. With no debt and no rent to pay, that should be plenty."

"You know what I would do, Dave?" Cathy suggested. "If she could live comfortably on $30,000, I would buy enough insurance to give her an income of $33,000. You know why? So she could continue the save-ten-percent program without cramping her lifestyle."

"You know, you kids aren't nearly as slow as your father says you are," Roy joshed. "That's great thinking, Cathy. Dave, I'm sure you'd agree that Sue deserves not only to live comfortably, but also to have the finer things in life. Well, you've learned how she can!"

"Thirty-three thousand it is," I concurred. "To create an investment income of $23,000 a year, assuming an eight percent interest rate, I would need how much, Roy?"

"Give or take a few hundred, you'd need $287,000. " James Murray intervened, proudly showing Clyde the calculator on his watch.

"As for inflation," I went on, "I really don't think I'd need that much. With Sue saving ten percent and with her likely, in fact certain, to reenter the travel agency business when the baby gets a little older, she should be fine." I looked around smugly.

"Excellent, Dave," Roy congratulated me. "The last bit on inflation was very well thought out. That's the type of analysis we all have to do on our insurance needs. It's imperative that we not buy too little insurance, but it's also important that we not buy too much. Did you total how much insurance you decided you needed? It would be $407,000 worth."

I was dumbfounded.

"He won't be able to afford his premiums, will he?" asked Tom, who, uncharacteristically, seemed genuinely concerned.

"I get $25,000 coverage free with my benefit package, but I'll still have to buy almost $400,000 worth. I'll need the insurance," I griped. "Paying the premiums is going to kill me!"

"Dave, my boy, you're wrong. If you buy the proper types of insurance, your premiums will be quite reasonable. For now, though, let's stick to the amounts and not get ahead of ourselves.

"Making the same assumptions . . . house, baby, et cetera . . . how much insurance should you place on Sue's life?" Roy then asked.

"Sue's no longer working at the travel agency, so our current family income would only drop by the $10,000 she makes selling her travel articles. But the expenses would also drop with one fewer person to support. With my income being fairly good, I'm going to say zero. No insurance on Sue's life."

"I can see your logic, Dave," Roy conceded.

"But . . ." I said, anticipating reservations.

"But I want to make two points. Always insure both spouses for at least the amount of the outstanding debt — in your case, $80,000. A debt-free balance sheet substantially reduces stress, along with freeing up cash flow. Raising a child, making payments on an $80,000 mortgage, and enjoying a good standard of living wouldn't be easy on your salary alone. Also, you've forgotten a couple of expenses that would result from Sue's death. One: funeral costs of $10,000; two: day care for your young child. With no debt, you won't need to replace the entire income from Sue's writing, I'll agree, but you want at least enough to cover the cost of child care."

"So I probably need $200,000 coverage on Sue," I surmised. "Eighty thousand to pay off the mortgage, $10,000 for the funeral and the rest to pay for a nanny for a few years."

"The point of all this was not just to help Dave." Roy motioned towards Tom and Cathy. "It's to help you two bored-looking individuals, as well. There may be a woman out there crazy enough to want Tom as a husband. There might be an even crazier man who would tolerate Dave as a brother-in-law. So eventually you may both be in the position of needing insurance. And when you are, you've got to be able to figure out exactly how much you need. All it takes is the knowledge I've given you — remembering the four needs for insurance proceeds — and some common sense."

"I'm going to talk to my brother about this tomorrow, Roy." Tom shook his head disbelievingly. "He's got two young children and a wife. I now know for a fact that he doesn't have nearly enough insurance. He has $150,000 coverage through work, but that's it."

"You may be doing him the biggest favour of his life . . . or at least doing his loved ones the biggest favour of _his_ life," replied Roy. "Now, before we move on to the different types of insurance, let me give you three illustrations of some tricky evaluations you may be faced with in the future.

"One: both spouses are working and making excellent money. That situation could arise, for example, if Cathy married a doctor. They analyze their insurance needs and decide that if either of them died, the other could carry on quite comfortably, at least financially, on his or her own without insurance proceeds. Their house is fully paid for and their two children could easily be supported on either parent's income. What's wrong with their analysis?"

For a few seconds, everyone was silent. Then I realized where Roy was headed. "What if they both die at the same time? Their children would be left with only the house."

"Excellent, Dave! Does everyone see? James, didn't you tell me about a case just like that?" Roy prodded.

"Yes. That happened to friends of Barb's parents several years ago. You have to protect against situations like that by buying a policy that pays only when both of the insureds die," answered James.

"All right. A second example," Roy continued without missing a beat as Tom got into the barber chair, "Cathy sells half of her business to Joe Schmoe. A year later, Joe dies, leaving his half to his wife, who has no business experience. She has no desire to enter the business world and decides that she wants to sell her half back to Cathy. Unfortunately, Cathy has no liquid reserves and has exhausted her lines of credit. Suddenly her life line, Richardson Landscaping, is in jeopardy. Will it be shut down? Will Schmoe's half be sold to an inappropriate person?"

"I should have had insurance on *his* life. Is that what you're saying?" asked Cathy.

"Yes. It's another example of how difficult it can be to analyze how much insurance to buy. It's not enough that you are properly insured so that your loved ones will be taken care of. You also have to make sure that anyone you're dependent on is properly insured."

Since I'm not dependent on anyone, this point didn't strike me as too important. It sure had an impact on Tom, though.

"Hey!" he blurted out, stopping Roy in midsnip. "Lucky you gave that example! If my brother were to die after we close our real estate deal, I'd be in trouble. I couldn't afford to pick up the payments on his half of the down-payment loan. I'm going to have to talk to him about us getting insurance on each other's life."

"Take care of that soon," Roy encouraged him. "One final example of insurance-needs analysis. Fifteen years from now, Tom has parlayed his monthly savings and apparent knack for buying undervalued properties into a $700,000 real estate empire. Unfortunately, he is hit by a bus." This drew applause from both Jimmy and Clyde. "Included in the $700,000 valuation is $300,000 worth of capital gains, which translates into a tax liability of approximately

$100,000. Tom felt he was self-insured, so the estate was limited to his personal residence, real estate holdings and baseball card collection. So his executor, Cathy, who incidentally was driving the bus" — this remark caused me to cough my Pepsi onto my white golf shorts — "is forced to sell a property to pay the tax bill. Sadly, real estate is at its lowest point in two decades, making it a terrible time to sell. But she has no choice. The point is that for liquidity reasons it would have been a good idea for Tom to carry enough insurance to cover his tax liability.

"I gave these three examples to show you that a lot of thought is needed to correctly analyze your insurance needs. Don't be lazy. Do the necessary thinking. Get a book out of the library. Talk to an insurance agent. They've had years of experience and have encountered almost every possible scenario. For heaven's sake, be insured for the correct amount! You owe it to yourself and to your family."

Tom's haircut was coming along nicely, and it was now obvious to everyone that Roy's promise of this month's lesson being shorter than last month's had a better-than-even chance of being broken. We hadn't even delved into the different types of insurance policies. I had nightmarish visions of Tom and me missing our tee-off time.

"Roy, I don't mean to sound unappreciative because I'm far from it. I can't believe how much we've learned again today, but Tom and I are supposed to meet Dad at Huron Oaks in less than an hour. With all the different types of policies still to be discussed, could we perhaps finish this off next month?"

"That won't be necessary, Dave. Although, as you pointed out, there are a number of different types of policies, there is only one that you, Cathy and Tom will probably ever need — *renewable and convertible term insurance*. It won't take me long to teach you why.

"I'm sure that even you three, with your limited financial backgrounds, have heard of the age-old argument of whole life versus term, better stated as cash-value insurance versus term insurance."

"I certainly have," remarked Cathy. "You won't believe this, but when I went to buy insurance last month, I actually decided to do a little research beforehand. All three books I read suggested that term insurance was a better alternative than cash-value insurance. Yet both agents I saw were very insistent that I buy cash-value. I bowed to their expertise and bought a *universal life* policy."

"I don't even know the difference," Tom admitted candidly.

James Murray leapt in, "Those agents recommended cash-value because — "

"Hold on, James," Roy ordered. "You'll have your chance. First, let's look at a couple of definitions.

"Term insurance is like fire insurance. It pays out the face amount of the policy if the insured dies, just as fire insurance pays out the face amount if the insured building burns down. Term insurance is in force for a stipulated length of time — or term — hence its name. It's most often sold in one-year, five-year, ten-year, or twenty-year terms. When the term expires, so does the insurance. There are no cash values, savings, or investment elements. It's insurance in its most basic and least expensive form.

"Cash-value insurance is basically a combination of term insurance and a forced-savings program, with the savings program being the cash-surrender value of the policy. Dave, are the odds of you dying next year if you own a cash-value insurance policy higher or lower than the odds of you dying next year if you own a term policy?"

"The same, of course. Even I know that."

"Yes, I think anyone could answer that question correctly. It's the significance of the answer that most people miss," Roy explained patiently.

Damn. He had lost me. "I'm not sure I follow you."

"I'm sure you've heard the expression, 'Buy term and invest the difference.' What does it mean to you?" Roy put the ball back in my court.

"Well, instead of buying a cash-value policy, you buy the same amount of term coverage, which is less expensive because it doesn't include a savings element. Then you invest the difference between the two costs in a savings vehicle."

"That's right. So, remembering your answer to the odds-of-dying question, what's wrong with the oft-heard question, 'Am I better to buy term and invest the difference or to buy a cash-value policy?' I'll tell you what's wrong. They are the same thing. As you said, the odds of dying are the same, regardless of what type of policy you buy. So there's really only one type of life insurance, and that is pure protection based on a mortality table. That's what term insurance is. Cash-value insurance is pure protection, or term insurance, plus a cash-value element. 'Buy term and invest the difference' is exactly what a cash-value policy does. The problem is, it doesn't invest that difference nearly as well as you can on your own."

"If that's the case, why do insurance companies issue cash-value products? And why do agents sell them?" asked Cathy.

"Because both companies and agents often put their own interests ahead of their clients'," James Murray responded hotly, before Roy had a chance to speak. "The premiums on cash-value policies are much higher — and so is the commission rate! The companies and agents make far more money by selling cash-value insurance than they could by selling term."

"You're pretty agitated, James!" Cathy exclaimed. "Do you agree with him, Roy?"

"No. With all due respect, James, I don't. Sure, there are a number of unscrupulous salespeople, but as I said earlier, I don't think it's any worse in the insurance industry than in any other business. Maybe it was fifteen years ago, when James was an agent. But now many agents do a conscientious job not only of placing insurance but also of estate and financial planning. The products have improved, and so have their prices. Now you can get price distinctions based on sex and based on smoking versus nonsmoking, for example. Professionalism is definitely on the rise, too. More and more agents are becoming better educated about all financial matters, not just insurance."

"If all that's true, why do they sell so much of what you claim is an inferior product?" Cathy persisted.

"Yes! If all that's true, why do they sell so much of what you claim is an inferior product?" James Murray echoed.

"The policy I just bought on my agent's recommendation was a cash-value policy," Cathy remarked, before Roy could offer a response.

"First, let me say that not all agents do push cash-value policies. Many have seen the light and now sell primarily renewable and convertible term insurance. Many are also espousing the benefits of paying yourself first, saving ten percent, and building a registered retirement savings plan. Those people are doing good jobs for their clients.

"Second, those who do sell cash-value insurance believe they are doing the right thing. They believe, and rightly so, that it is vital not only to have the proper amount of coverage, but also to become self-insured through saving and investing. For obvious reasons, insurance costs increase dramatically later in life. So you have to have saved the funds necessary to pay them, or to have saved enough not to even need insurance in your later years. Most agents feel a cash-value policy accomplishes this goal of saving while at the same time insuring you.

"They argue that although 'Buy term and invest the difference' sounds good in theory, it seldom works in practice. Why? Because for most people the more accurate expression is 'Buy term and spend the difference.' Agents see that a lot of clients don't have the discipline or the knowledge to invest the difference. So even though they start out properly insured with inexpensive term coverage, they end up facing a retirement that includes high insurance costs and an empty bank account."

"Do most people end up that way?" I wondered.

"Unfortunately, a lot do. It's staggering the number of people over the age of fifty-five who are in serious financial trouble. But you won't be," Roy assured us.

"How can you be so certain?"

"Because you're getting financial advice from the wealthy barber. Between your ten percent fund and your retirement planning, you'll be self-insured at a very reasonable age — very reasonable. You're not only buying term and investing the difference, but you're also investing more. And you're investing it well!"

"That sounds great, Roy. But if the insurance company is offering to do it all for you by selling cash-value insurance — insurance plus savings — why not let them? Won't they do a better job investing than we would, anyway?"

Cathy's question seemed justified.

"No!" was Roy's resounding answer. "Normally, the savings portions of cash-value policies are comparatively poor investments! Tom, if I came to you and said the following, would you save with me? 'To save at our institution, you must buy life insurance. You must pay for it even if you don't need it. We'll take everything you deposit in the first year for ourselves.

In future years, we'll charge you to deposit money into your savings account. You can borrow the money at any time, but we'll charge you interest. If you happen to die while this loan is outstanding, we'll decrease the amount we were to pay your beneficiary by the outstanding amount of the loan. If you don't borrow from this account and you die, we'll pay the beneficiary only the face amount of the policy — we'll keep your savings for ourselves. Oh, and finally, we don't offer the greatest rates of return.'"

"No, thanks. I think I'll keep buying houses with my brother. You know, I always thought it was too good to be true that you could often borrow from your insurance policy at a low interest rate. But paying any interest to borrow your own money isn't that good a deal, is it?"

"Say, Tommy boy. If you thought being able to borrow your own money from your policy at five percent was a good deal, you'll love my offer," James Murray wheedled facetiously. "I'll lend you your money out of your bank account and only charge you four percent! Sounds good, eh?"

"You see," Roy went on, "the deal I offered Tom isn't far removed from the deal offered by the traditional cash-value policy. In a way, you can't blame insurance companies for trying to make money. They have to cover expenses, pay their agents, and make a profit for their shareholders. That can't leave much for you, the policyholder. To save successfully, you have to cut out the middleman — "

"And you have to invest for growth," a fervent Tom interrupted.

"A good point, indeed. As we saw last month, the last thing we want is our long-term savings tied up earning low rates of return. We want to be owners, not loaners," Roy reminded us.

"You mentioned that if we buy a traditional cash-value policy and die, all we get back is the face value of the insurance we have paid for. The insurance company keeps our savings. That seems almost illegal," I remarked.

"That's one point on which James and I are in full agreement," Roy sighed. "For years, the insurance companies virtually stole the savings of many of their policyholders. In fact, some companies still issue policies that keep the savings portion on the death of the insured. That's not fair, and there's no defence for it. Fortunately, most agents and companies are getting away from that type of product."

"The premium you pay for those policies covers the costs of two services: protection for your dependants if you should die, and protection for yourself if you should live. You pay dearly for both those services, but unless you've mastered the impossible trick of being simultaneously alive and dead, you're restricted to receiving the benefits of only one service. It's a terrible deal!" pointed out James Murray.

"There is one other point I'd like to make here. Some agents agree that cash-value policies might not be the best way to save, but argue that they're still worthwhile because they're compulsory savings plans. That," Roy snorted, "is nonsense. If you have the self-discipline to make premium payments over a long period of time, you certainly have the self-discipline to manage a suitable savings program on your own. In fact, you three have already started."

"I'm confused by one thing." Cathy stared at Roy intently. "The cash-value policy I bought last week was a lot different from the traditional one you two are describing. It's called universal life, and my agent assures me that the rates of return are very competitive. He also told me that, when I die, my beneficiary gets both the insurance proceeds and the policy's savings component. In fact, I can even invest the savings in a vehicle similar to a mutual fund if I want to. That doesn't sound like a bad deal, does it?"

"Universal life is a great example of what I said earlier. The insurance industry really has improved its product line over the past few years. Universal life is a much better product than the traditional whole life policy. It unbundles the insurance and savings elements, meaning that when you die, as you said, your beneficiary will receive both. It also offers more competitive rates of return. That being said, though, for a couple of reasons it still isn't as good as buying term and investing the difference. First, the term insurance component may be purchased much more cheaply outside the package. Second, because the company has to cover expenses and make a profit, the investment/savings portion will not yield as great a return inside the package as outside. This is especially true if you cash in the policy in the early years, as the insurance company's fixed costs on each policy are very high. If, for example, after ten years you cancel your universal life policy because you no longer need the insurance, the rate of return on your savings component is usually only in the three percent area — which is ridiculous.

"Universal life does have one major benefit, and that is that, at the moment, the savings portion is allowed to grow tax-deferred. However, it's still not as mathematically sound as buying term and maximizing your RRSP, or buying term and paying off your non-deductible debt, or, when you're young, buying term and investing for long-term growth.

"Cash-value policies carry level premiums, whereas term becomes more expensive as you get older. Why is that?" Roy tested us.

"I know," Tom stated. "It's because, with cash-value policies, you overpay in the early years to subsidize the rising costs in the later years. The overpayment is invested and compounded so the rising costs in later years are easily covered."

"Tom, I'm impressed." Roy's compliment was genuine. "Is this a good thing?"

Tom spoke up again. "No. It's nonsense, as James would say. Why overpay in the early years when there's a good chance you won't even need the coverage in the later years? I'll be self-insured by the time my term insurance costs become expensive. Also, when you're younger you need the money more. You have more responsibilities. It's a bad time to be overpaying for insurance."

"Tom, I take back all the things I've thought about you over the years. You're definitely smarter than the average bear," remarked Roy.

"Bear, perhaps, but not human," I muttered, belying the fact that I was impressed.

"Okay. I see that term insurance is the way to go, but what about my agent's argument that buying insurance now was a good idea so I would guarantee future insurability?" Cathy absent-mindedly pushed a fallen lock of hair with her toe. "That seems to make sense, doesn't it? Why did James label that as nonsense?"

"I'll answer that, Roy," James Murray offered. "*Nonsense* might not have been the right word. Maybe it's a little strong. But I still don't think you should buy life insurance unless you need it. I believe an infinitesimal percentage of people are turned down for life insurance when they first apply for it. Yes, there is a chance you might become one of them, but there's also a chance you'll be in a car accident today. I'm sure you'll still drive. In life, you can't avoid all risks. If you do insist on buying to guarantee insurability, though, make sure you buy term insurance so that, for the same premium dollars you can guarantee as much insurability as possible."

"Very diplomatically spoken, James," Roy said, smiling. "I'll hurry along so you two can make your golf game."

"Yeah. If we miss that tee-off time, you'll wish you had insurance," Tom advised Roy with a wink.

"I mentioned the terms *renewable* and *convertible* earlier. Renewable means that at the expiry of the stated term you can renew the insurance without having to prove insurability by taking a medical. It's obvious why that's important. If you got cancer but weren't going to die before your term insurance expired, guaranteed renewability would be your salvation.

"It's often a wise move when you purchase renewable term insurance to ensure that your policy sets out the maximum rate that you can be charged on each of your future renewal dates. Why? To prevent the issuing company from allowing you to renew only at uncompetitive rates. Whether those uncompetitive rates arise through company design or are caused by some other phenomenon — AIDS, for example — you won't be protected unless your policy has guaranteed future premium costs.

"Usually, you're allowed to renew until age sixty-five or seventy. This will be more than sufficient for you three, because you'll all be self-insured long before then.

"Convertible means that the policyholder has the right to convert the face amount of the policy to any cash-value plan sold by the issuing company, again without proving insurability. This feature is important in case you need insurance past age sixty-five and can no longer renew your term insurance. I doubt if any of you will have to call on this feature, but buy it just the same. It's very cheap," Roy finished.

"I feel very strongly that no company should be allowed to sell nonrenewable or nonconvertible term insurance. The reasons are self-evident," remarked James Murray. "There are just too many ways the policyholder can get hurt."

"Also, when you buy your term policy, always buy *nonparticipating* insurance. *Always*. Participating policies work like this. The issuing company adds a surcharge to your premium. Out of this surcharge, they pay you *dividends*. These are not dividends in the normal sense of the word — a partial distribution of after-tax profits. Instead, they are just rebates of surcharges. By law, the insurance companies cannot guarantee the amounts of the future dividend payments. Those amounts will be determined by the actuarial success of the company. Really, a participating policy is nothing more than a way in which the insurance company gets you, as a policyholder, to share the risk. No one should buy insurance to share risk. We buy it to attempt to eliminate risk. Don't buy a participating policy!" Roy emphasized.

"Should we shop the market for the lowest rate?" was Cathy's next question.

"Yes," James Murray replied.

"No," Roy countered. "You should always attempt to get a competitive rate, but not necessarily the lowest rate. Many agents are restricted to offering only the products of the company they're licensed with. If you are dealing with such an agent, and he or she is doing a good job helping you to analyze your insurance needs and giving you other financial planning advice, it is probably prudent to stick with that agent. This may mean not getting the lowest rate. Your rate, however, should still be a competitive one. Too much loyalty can be expensive!

"It's important to note that you probably won't be buying all your term insurance from an agent. There are two other potentially excellent sources. One is mortgage death insurance. Many savings institutions now offer inexpensive term insurance that will pay off your mortgage with them in the event of your death. Dave, when you get your mortgage next year, you will probably want to buy that coverage. If either Susan or you should die, the insurance will pay off the outstanding balance of your mortgage. The cost of the insurance, often the cheapest available, is added to the monthly cost of your mortgage. It's an excellent product, but it's not always less expensive than an individual term insurance policy. Check the rates.

"A second nonagent source of term insurance is the group insurance offered through work. Cathy, this won't apply to you at this point. Group insurance can, and I stress *can*, be a great deal. Because it is distributed to the consumer more efficiently, group insurance is often an inexpensive alternative to an individual policy. There are some caveats with group insurance, though. It isn't always better than an individual policy. Group rates are based on the average person within the group. If you are substantially younger than your colleagues, you may be better off with an individual policy. Likewise, if you are female and the group policy has no distinction based on sex, or if you are a nonsmoker and the group policy has no distinction based on smoking. Get your group-rate quote from your company's personnel department and then get a quote from your agent for the costs of an individual policy. Go with the least expensive. It's just common sense. Also, if you leave your company, you may not be able to take your insurance with you on a convertible and renewable basis. That's not a good situation. Instead, almost all group policies allow you to convert to a cash-value plan within thirty-one days of leaving the group. We don't want cash-value, so only accept this conversion if you are unable to qualify for individual term insurance at the time of your departure.

"Also, don't restrict your analysis of group policies

to the one offered at your place of work. You may be able to qualify for a plan available through your university alumni, a fraternal society, or a union. Some of these plans are excellent."

"Tom's a card-carrying member of the Archie Fan Club. Do they have a group policy?" Cathy teased.

"I'm offered $25,000 coverage free at work. Should I take it?" I asked.

"Two months and that's our first stupid question. Not bad. Not bad. Take anything you can get free, Dave," Roy replied, shaking his head.

"How much does term insurance cost?" I queried, hoping not to embarrass myself again.

"Let's look at your example, Dave. We decided that next year you'll need around $400,000 coverage, and Sue will need $200,000. Well, using the $25,000 you get as a benefit, inexpensive mortgage death insurance and properly selected renewable and convertible term — I'm guessing a little — but you're probably looking at about eighty dollars a month."

"That's it?" I was amazed. "I thought it would be hundreds a month."

"No. Term insurance is a bargain, no doubt about it. And the nice thing is that as you get older and your cost per thousand dollars of coverage goes up, you'll have less need for insurance," Roy explained. "Your living estate will be increasing each year."

"What about disability insurance, Roy? Do I need it?"

"We'll talk about disability insurance in an upcoming lesson, Cathy."

"Next month?"

"No. Next month we're going to look at registered retirement savings plans — RRSPs."

"Should we bring our sleeping bags next month, Roy? It's almost Sunday, isn't it?" Tom kidded, as we headed for the door.

"All I'm doing for you three and that's how you

treat me . . . Oh, the disrespectful youth of today. Hey, you two should score a little better this time out."

"Why's that?"

"It's after eleven o'clock. You're going to miss the first three holes."

"Ooh, wealthy and witty. What a deadly combination." I grinned, as we stepped back out into the sunlight.

"Don't worry about it." Tom patted me on the shoulder. "By the time we get to the course, your dad will have paid for our greens fees. Now, *that's* sound financial planning!"

▌6▐
OUR RSP

"Good morning, dear friends," Roy greeted us enthusiastically. "What a fabulous day!"

"Actually, it's overcast and cool," I noted, looking to Tom and Cathy for verification.

"I'm talking about the positively glowing feeling permeating every fibre of one's being the day after a Tiger ninth-inning comeback victory." Roy beamed.

"You're making me sick" came from the recesses of the back room, where Clyde was stewing, and brewing coffee.

"How right you are, Roy." I smiled. "On days like this, it's just great to be alive."

"We're going down to tomorrow's game," Cathy informed him cheerfully. "Sue and Dave, and Tom and I. Oh, let me rephrase that. I'm going with Sue and Dave, and Tom is also coming."

"And to think I was going to pay for your ticket," sighed Tom, shaking his head.

"On a more serious note, does each of you have a photocopied bill to show me?" Roy asked, referring to last month's ultimatum to *get a will or else.*

Cathy had the honour of handing him all three documents.

"I'm impressed," he praised us. "You three really seem determined to get your financial affairs in order. I commend you."

"Not that we have much choice," I rejoined.

"As I pointed out last month, when it comes to proper estate distribution, the importance of a will cannot be overstated. Where there's a will, there's a way."

Groan.

"You've been dying to use that line, haven't you, Roy? No pun intended," Tom added. "I'll bet you meant to use it last month, forgot, and spent the past four weeks in a state of depression. Right?"

"Of course not, Tom. It was a spontaneous, off-the-cuff remark," answered Roy, with a wink at James Murray.

"Before we get started with this month's lesson, I want to tell all of you that I cancelled my life insurance policy," Cathy announced proudly. "Mind you, right after I told my agent, I regretted my decision."

"Why?" James Murray asked curiously.

"Because I thought he was going to kill me," Cathy said, chuckling.

"Yeah. Some salespeople don't handle rejection well. Did he ask you why you had changed your mind?"

"Yes, and when I explained all the reasons, he became quite indignant and said, 'A little knowledge is a dangerous thing.'"

"To which you replied?" I prompted her.

"To which I replied, 'You're right, so why don't you take some courses?'"

"That conduct is not indicative of most insurance agents' attitudes," Roy commented once the laughter had subsided. "As I said last month, for the most part they're a very professional group. That particular agent was probably upset because he mistakenly believed that he was acting in your best interests, and he was frustrated when you dismissed his advice."

"Bull," James Murray snorted. "He was annoyed that he had lost a commission."

"That too," Roy conceded. "Whatever his reason, his behaviour was out of line and, as I said, not representative of insurance agents' behaviour in general. Anyway, you did the right thing, Cathy. You have to do what's best for you, not what's best for the agent. If that means cancelling or replacing a policy, so be it."

"If you want to replace an insurance policy because you've found a less expensive alternative, or because you're making the often intelligent move from a cash-value policy to a term policy, there is an important caveat to keep in mind. You shouldn't cancel the old policy until you have purchased the new one, just in case you're no longer insurable," James Murray explained from behind the sports section of the *Globe and Mail.*

"Good point, James!" Tom exclaimed. "I'll have to mention that to my brother. He's going to switch to a renewable and convertible term insurance policy and do his saving on his own."

"Speaking of Brian, how's the real estate deal coming along? Have you closed yet?"

"Yeah. We closed two weeks ago. We hadn't budgeted very well for some of the closing costs. Actually, we hadn't budgeted for them at all," Tom confessed. "Appraisal fees, title search, legal costs . . . all that stuff adds up! But everything worked out fine in the end, and Kyle and Cindy moved in last Saturday. The three of us couldn't believe all the little improvements my brother had made to the place. He'd spent less than $1,000, but the house looked as if he'd put $10,000 into it. Things like a bit of new trim make all the difference in the world. The guy is amazing."

"Sounds great, Tom," Roy remarked. "It really is incredible what a handyman — "

"Handyperson," Cathy corrected.

"Handyperson," Roy acknowledged, "can accomplish with relatively little money. It looks as though Brian is the ideal partner. Did you two discuss your insurance needs?"

"We each bought a renewable and convertible term insurance policy, with a face value of $25,000, naming the other as beneficiary. If either of us dies, the survivor will be able to pay off our entire down-payment loan. Now it won't cause me any financial hardship if Brian happens to die. In fact, I'm encouraging him to take up hang gliding," Tom joked.

"Good thinking, Tom. Not the hang-gliding part, but the insurance. You're a surprisingly quick study," Roy reflected.

"What do you mean *surprisingly*?" Tom sputtered.

"Today, we're going to look at registered retirement savings plans," Roy continued, rendering Tom's question rhetorical. "RRSPs present a tremendous opportunity to many Canadians. All of us have to save for retirement, and there is simply no better vehicle than an RRSP."

"I prefer an RX7," James Murray murmured in the background.

"Statistics show that many Canadians retire near — or under — the poverty level. In fact, it's said that over fifty percent of retired Canadians *need* some form of government assistance to survive. That such a situation exists in a country enjoying our level of economic prosperity is nothing short of embarrassing. Nowhere is Canadians' lack of financial acumen more glaringly evident. With our aging population and the fact that many experts now question the long-term stability of the Canada Pension Plan, it's more important now than ever for Canadians to save properly for their 'golden years.'

"Let's assume a certain successful female entrepreneur was due to retire tomorrow. We'll call her . . .

Cathy." Roy smiled. "Let's also assume that she has been making $100,000 a year. How much would she need to have saved to bring in that same annual income in retirement?"

"Making our standard assumption of an eight percent guaranteed return, she would need $1,250,000," replied Tom, without even using James Murray's watch calculator. "One million two hundred and fifty thousand dollars," he repeated slowly, with a low whistle.

After our second lesson, I thought I had become accustomed to bandying about large numbers. However, I'll have to admit that our *imaginary* Cathy's need for one and a quarter million dollars to maintain her lifestyle floored me. "That's an astronomical amount of money!" I gasped.

"It sure is," Roy agreed. "To maintain one's customary lifestyle in retirement demands a phenomenal amount of savings. That's why an RRS — "

"Nowadays, aren't most people members of pension plans? And what about our ten percent fund? Won't it provide much of our needed capital?" interrupted Tom, whose financial confidence level was rising by the minute.

"Good questions, Tom. Very good questions. And now is probably as good a time as any to address them.

"First, regarding pension plans. A great number of people are not members of a pension plan. Professionals, commissioned salespeople, small-business owners, for example . . . Most of the time, people from these occupations are pensionless, if there is such a word. In addition, many employees of small businesses, in fact many employees of every size of business, are not participants in a pension plan. For all those people, it's imperative to set aside money for retirement. Besides the people who are not involved in a pension plan at all, many others are members of pension plans that on the members' retirement will not provide them with suitable incomes.

"Both you and Dave have outstanding plans at your places of work. Both of you will retire to a pension income in the area of sixty-five percent of your last working year's income. But you two are the exception, not the rule. Most pension plans don't provide nearly that well for their members."

"So you're saying that Dave and I don't need RRSPs, but that many other people, including Cathy, do?" Tom inferred.

"No. I'm not saying that at all. It should be every Canadian's goal to have an after-tax income at retirement equivalent to his or her last working year's income. That being the case, you two boys will still need to save enough money to bring in the thirty-five percent difference between your pension income and your last working year's income."

"Why?" challenged Tom. "Everything you read says that less income is needed in retirement. You usually don't have a mortgage anymore. Nine times out of ten, you no longer have dependent children. Your house is fully furnished. If you've saved properly, you've stopped having to buy insurance. Obviously, expenses are way down in retirement. So why do you need as much money as you did in your last years of work?"

This question seemed very reasonable to me, and apparently to Cathy, too, as she nodded sagely.

"At first glance, what you said seems to be logical, but there are some flaws in your argument.

"In most cases, several years before retirement, the mortgage has been paid off, and the children have moved out. So for many, the last few years at work are characterized by high income levels and significantly reduced expenses. In all likelihood, disposable income is at its highest point ever. It's no fun having to lower your standard of living at retirement because of a drop in your income. Psychologically, it's a difficult, if not traumatic, adjustment.

"If the decline in expenses happened to coincide perfectly with the date of retirement instead of occurring earlier, I don't believe there would be a major problem. But it seldom does. Adjusting to a fairly dramatic drop in your disposable income is not my idea of a good way to start retired life. Especially since it's a *myth* that present-day retired people spend much less money on lifestyle than their working counterparts. People don't retire and head straight to the rocking chair. While the rest of us are slaving away, many retirees are playing golf, taking up hobbies, travelling extensively, and participating in a myriad of other activities that all have one common denominator — they cost money!

"Another thing you have to keep in mind is our old friend — inflation. Many pensions are not adjusted each year to reflect the rising costs of living, that is, they are not *indexed*. Others are not fully indexed. They may have a cap of a four or eight percent annual increase in benefits. If inflation were to hover at ten percent for a number of years, the receivers of non-indexed or partially indexed pensions could find themselves in trouble. Hundreds of thousands of people were caught in this bind in the early eighties.

"Also, there are a couple of major expenditures that sometimes arise in retirement that can be very costly . . . very difficult to cope with on a pension . . . even a good pension. Sadly, deteriorating health goes hand in hand with advancing age. There are any number of medical costs that can cause your financial health to decline right along with your physical health.

"And yes, admittedly you will probably no longer have dependent children — but what about dependent parents? As I've said many times, Canadians are, for the most part, financial illiterates. You three are learning the right things to do, but many people aren't as fortunate, including many parents. Oftentimes, elderly parents become dependent on financial help from their children."

"My dad threatens me with that scenario daily," I added with a smile.

"Your years in retirement should be among the best years of your life. So you owe it to yourself to do everything possible now to enable you to enjoy fully those later years. That means saving enough money in your working years to enable you to maintain your income in retirement," Roy concluded.

"You've made some thought-provoking points, Roy, but as Tom asked earlier, won't our ten percent fund take care of our income problems? In May, you guaranteed us that someday we'd be wealthy," I reminded him.

"Yes, and I back that guarantee 100 percent. But the ten percent fund is not intended to augment our retirement income. It's our I've-made-it-big money. It's our I-can-now-do-and-buy-anything-I-want capital. A mansion on the lake, a Florida condominium, fancy cars . . . these are the reasons we're saving ten percent of everything we make," Roy responded emphatically.

"But surely we'll have so much that if we happened to be a bit short on the income side, we could always tap our ten percent fund, couldn't we?" Cathy asked meekly.

"Ah, but we'd prefer not to, Ms. Richardson," Roy the Professor chided. "Ideally, if we save properly for retirement, we won't have to. Let's refer again to our imaginary professional. If Cathy retired tomorrow, but had saved only enough to give her an income of $50,000 a year, she would have two options. She would either have to live on about half of what she was accustomed to or dip into her ten percent fund to make up the difference. She wouldn't have to dip into it for just $50,000, though. She'd have to use $625,000 of her fund, because it would take that amount, invested at eight percent, to create a $50,000 annual cash flow. Suddenly, our finer-things-in-life money is being depleted dramatically. For every one dollar of income, twelve dollars and fifty cents must be used from the ten percent fund," Roy explained.

"Eight percent of twelve and a half being one," I calculated.

"And your dad said you were a 'math murderer,'" Roy kidded.

"I see your point, Roy, and I agree. I'm sure these two do, too," Cathy assumed correctly, motioning at Tom and me. "So you're saying we should save ten percent and invest it for growth *and* save enough money separately to assure us of maintaining our preretirement income."

"That's precisely what I'm saying. To be in truly great shape, you must do both."

"Once again, Roy, your argument makes perfect sense. Nobody could question its logic, but is it feasible? I mean, saving ten percent and saving for retirement, too, could be pretty difficult! With that on top of rent, groceries, and all the routine costs of life in the twentieth century, I'll be cleaned out. I won't be able to leave my apartment!"

Tom had raised yet another valid point. I suspected Roy might have a tough time answering it satisfactorily.

"As you have learned through your own experience during the past two months, saving the ten percent isn't that difficult. By paying yourself first, it's almost painless. Have any of you missed the money or noticed a decline in your standard of living?" Roy demanded.

"No" was the unanimous response.

"But now you're also expecting us to save for retirement — "

"Whoa! Hold on, Tom. Saving hundreds of thousands of dollars for your retirement may sound intimidating, but it really isn't. Remember, you three have discovered the magic of compound interest. Once again, this time within an RRSP, it's going to be our closest friend. That shouldn't surprise you. But what might surprise you is the identity of another helpful new friend — the government."

"It's no friend of mine, Roy," Tom insisted. "I give it a hefty portion of everything I make, and in return it loses my mail."

"In the case of RRSPs, it really is your friend," Roy assured him. "As you'll see in a minute, the government subsidizes your RRSP contributions, in some cases by almost fifty percent. In addition, it allows funds within your RRSP to grow tax-free until they're withdrawn. This is a fantastic benefit.

"Between the government assistance and the savings that you will realize by purchasing term insurance instead of cash-value insurance, your RRSP contributions will be largely financed without you having to do any additional saving. You will have to do some, of course, but it will be a reasonable amount. And if we use our old trick of paying ourselves first, we'll hardly notice it. True?" Roy directed to Jimmy, James Murray and Clyde.

"True," the trio pronounced solemnly.

"How exactly does the government subsidize contributions?" I questioned.

"All in good time, Dave . . . all in good time. First, let me explain exactly what an RRSP is.

"Knowledgeable people have long realized that they must save for their retirements. Retirement savings plans, RSPs, have been a part of financial planning for hundreds of years. Saving some of today's income to provide for tomorrow's needs is essential and not new. Unfortunately, statistics have shown over and over that most Canadians believe that somehow the financial element of retirement will take care of itself. Many others who do understand the importance of saving for retirement do not have the discipline to set aside money accordingly. That's understandable. It's not easy for people in their twenties, thirties, or even their forties to worry about life in their late fifties and sixties. It seems so far away.

"Years ago, the government realized that it was faced with not only an undisciplined and somewhat uninformed work force, but also with a rapidly aging population. Clearly, something had to be done. And say what you will about our government, in the 1950s it did something very creative and very wise to motivate people to save for retirement. It added a second *R* to RSP. *R* for Registered. If you register your plan and follow the government's rules and guidelines, you are allowed to deduct your registered savings from your taxable income, and all the money within your RRSP is allowed to grow tax-free until withdrawn. An inspired idea!

"Let's say Dave contributes $1,000 to his RRSP this year. That $1,000 is deducted from his taxable income, meaning, with his *marginal tax rate* being approximately forty percent, that he will get back $400 in the form of tax savings. He will have $1,000 in his RRSP, but will be only $600 out of pocket."

"What's a marginal tax rate?" I asked, hoping Tom wouldn't show me up by answering.

"It's the percentage that is paid to Revenue Canada of the last dollar you make in a year. It's a very important term to understand. If Joe Blow makes $40,000 during a calendar year and pays $10,000 in taxes, his absolute tax rate is twenty-five percent. However, his marginal tax rate is substantially higher. It's the rate of tax he would pay on his next dollar of income or, to look at it another way, the rate at which he would avoid taxes if he reduced his taxable income by a dollar," Roy explained.

"So if you're in the highest marginal tax bracket, the government subsidizes almost half of your contribution," Cathy pointed out.

"With the new tax reform, not half, but yes, almost. It re — "

"I'm going to contribute as much as I can afford," an excited Tom interjected.

"There are limits on how much you can contribute annually, Tom," cautioned an apparently well-informed Cathy.

"That's right, Tom," Roy concurred. "There's a limit to our government's unprecedented generosity. They have tried and I think for the most part have succeeded in developing contribution limits that, one, offer a solid incentive to save without devastating the government's tax revenues, and two, take into account a potential contributor's pension involvement. Obviously, someone who is not involved in a pension plan is going to have to save more for retirement through an RRSP than someone who is. Similarly, someone making $25,000 a year is not going to have to save as much to maintain his or her lifestyle in retirement as is someone who makes $100,000 a year. The limits reflect all this."

"What are the limits?"

"This year the maximum allowable contribution is $12,500 or eighteen percent of your income last year, whichever is less," Roy began.

"Last year's income?" I interrupted.

"That's right," Roy responded patiently. "Your allowable contributions are now determined by your previous year's income. This creates some interesting opportunities . . . and problems. For example, let's suppose Dave gets a sabbatical leave for the next calendar year. Even though he'd have no earned income, he'd still qualify to make an RRSP contribution based on his current year's income."

"Problem is, I'd have no money," I noted, chuckling.

"Precisely," Roy confirmed. "And what's more, in the following year, when you're working again and, therefore, do have money, you won't be eligible to make a contribution. Of course, careful planning and good saving habits can combine to overcome these timing problems."

"Great," added Tom sarcastically.

"On the positive side," Roy continued, "the fact that your allowable RRSP contribution is based on your previous year's income means that you'll now be able to contribute to your plan in your first year of retirement."

"Interesting point," James Murray interjected. "I'll bet a lot of people haven't realized that."

"Aren't the limits going to increase annually?" Cathy asked.

"That's right, Cathy. Each year from 1994 to 1996, inclusive, the limit will rise by $1,000. Then, starting in '97, the limits will rise each year to reflect wage inflation."

"Those new limits are great!"

"Not so fast, Dave," Roy cautioned me. "The limits are reduced by a new calculation called a 'pension adjustment.' The 'P.A. amount,' as it's called, reflects an attempt by the government to make sure we're all on a level playing-field. In other words, the better your pension plan, the higher your P.A., and, therefore, the lower your allowable RRSP contribution. If you have a rich pension plan — for example, Dave's — the P.A. will then reduce, or, in some instances, even eliminate the amount you can contribute to RRSPs."

"I'm not a member of a pension plan," Cathy noted.

"P.A. of zero," was Roy's concise response. "And, Tom, before you ask, your P.A. will be high because your pension is reasonable, but not nearly as high as Dave's."

"How do we figure out our P.A.s?"

"You don't. It's too complex for us common folk. Your personnel department will provide your P.A."

"Roy," Cathy said, continuing her barrage of questions, "what's this new 'carry-forward provision' all about?"

Tom and I just shook our heads.

"I'm simplifying a bit, but basically the carry-forward provision is a new policy that allows taxpayers to make up contributions that they did not make in earlier years and to obtain a full tax deduction for up to seven years, and sometimes longer. For example, if Cathy didn't make any of her eligible $12,500 contribution this year, she could then contribute $26,000 next year."

"That's a great deal, isn't it, Roy?"

"Perhaps," Roy mused, "but I hope people don't overuse the carry-forward provision. Unfortunately, it actually encourages our already-biggest problem — procrastination. Remember, it's still important to get the money into the RRSP as soon as possible, so it can grow tax-free."

"Plus, if it's tough to find $10,000 one year, it may be even harder to find $20,000 the next," Tom reasoned, as I got down from Roy's chair.

"It will be hard for you to save all that money each year, Sis."

"Dave, I can see why — " Roy began.

"Can I field that one, Roy?" Cathy asked eagerly. "I had the same reservations myself, Dave, when I decided for the first time to contribute to my limit of $7,500. But because the government subsidized me for about half of the needed amount, my out-of-pocket expenses were only about $310 a month. That may sound like a lot, but bear in mind two things. One: I must humbly remind you that I make a very good income; two: I didn't have any money coming off my pay cheque each month for a pension. To top it all off, I had the money go directly from my bank account to my RRSP each month. I paid myself first, and so I barely missed it. That's why it didn't come as any surprise to me when the same held true for my ten percent savings."

"Beautiful, intelligent, witty, and soon to be very wealthy . . . I wish I were young again," Roy complimented my sister.

"Start now . . . that's the key," Roy continued. "There's such a compelling reason to start now."

"Compound interest," Tom anticipated him.

"Compound interest, indeed," an impressed Roy confirmed. "As I said two months ago, time can be your greatest ally. The combination of time and compound interest is more powerful than a locomotive, a nuclear reaction, or even a Cecil Fielder home run. John D. Rockefeller often spoke of the magic of compound interest. He once said, 'If you want to become really wealthy, you must have your money work for you. The amount you get paid for your personal effort is relatively small compared with the amount you can earn by having your money make money.' He knew whereof he spoke.

"Twenty-two-year-old twins decide to start saving for retirement," Roy offered as an example. "One opens an RRSP, invests $2,000 a year for six years, and then stops. His RRSP compounds at twelve percent a year. The second twin procrastinates and doesn't open an RRSP until the seventh year — the year his brother stopped. He then contributes $2,000 a year for thirty-seven years. He, too, earns a rate of twelve percent a year. At age sixty-five, they go out for dinner to compare their RRSP holdings. The second twin, who is fully aware that his brother stopped contributing thirty-seven years earlier, is confident that his RRSP will be worth at least ten times as much. What do you think, Cathy?"

"I think he's wrong . . . or you wouldn't be telling us the story," was her clever rationale.

"Yeah, yeah," Roy said, laughing. "At age sixty-five, they would each have approximately $1,200,000."

Despite Cathy's glib response, the significance of Roy's point was not lost on any of us. It was a vivid example of the effect of compound interest and hard-hitting testimony to the benefits of starting one's RRSP early.

"Let's move on to the different investment options —"

"I just have one quick question, Roy," I interrupted. "A number of the people I work with never started an RRSP and now, because of the amount they're putting into their pensions, they aren't allowed to contribute much. How should they save for their retirement so they can maintain their income?"

"Good question, Dave. The answer is simple. They should save more than ten percent of their income. Not a lot more, but more . . . say, fifteen percent. On retirement, one-third of their ten percent fund should be used to augment their income," was his concise answer.

"You mean their fifteen percent fund," I corrected him.

"Right you are," Roy acknowledged. "Now, on to investing. There are a number of different ways you can invest your RRSP contributions. Eligible investments include cash, Canada Savings Bonds, Treasury Bills, Canadian corporate and government bonds, guaranteed investment certificates, shares listed on prescribed Canadian stock exchanges, mutual funds that fulfill content qualifications, and even your own mortgage. In addition, you can hold certain foreign investments, as long as eighty-two percent, on a cost basis, of all property held in your RRSP is Canadian."

"Why do we have to have eighty-two percent of our RRSP invested in Canada?"

"There's a huge pool of capital in RRSPs now, and it's growing larger each year. For obvious reasons, the government wants that money to stay in Canada," Roy said patiently. "Eighteen percent foreign content doesn't sound like much, but I highly recommend you take advantage of it for two reasons. It makes sense from a diversification standpoint, and it also increases the number of opportunities available — that normally increases the long-term rate of return."

"Most of what I've read says that you should invest your RRSP dollars in guaranteed products. 'Be a loaner,' as Roy would say. The experts recommend buying things like Canada Savings Bonds and guaranteed investment certificates." Cathy looked up from a sketch that she was doing of the interior of Roy's barbershop. "Right, Roy?"

Tom seemed perplexed for the first time that day. "What? I thought it was better to be an owner!"

"The experts point out that because all RRSP deposits are allowed to grow tax-free until withdrawn, there is no tax advantage afforded to capital gains. In essence, growth and interest are taxed equally, that is, not at all, at least not until withdrawal, when the RRSP proceeds are subject to tax as they are deregistered through the use of an annuity or a registered retirement income fund," Cathy replied.

Now I was confused. "Registered retirement income fund?"

"Forget you heard that term, Dave," Roy advised me, shaking his head. "You're at least twenty-five years away from needing to learn about RRIFs and annuities . . . and by then the government will have changed the rules dozens of times. Cathy's point does merit some consideration, though.

"Many experts do feel that RRSP investors should confine their investments to guaranteed products because capital gains do not receive preferential tax treatment in an RRSP. I don't agree. Are guaranteed investments the only way to go just because interest and capital gains are treated equally from a tax perspective? Say you're convinced that through well-planned ownership you can achieve an average rate of return of thirteen percent per year. Are you going to buy Canada Savings Bonds or guaranteed investment certificates paying seven or eight percent, just because everything is taxed equally? Of course not!

"My RRSP has averaged close to thirteen percent over the years through a combination of ownership, patience and dollar cost averaging. People who have been loaners may have averaged eight percent. Does it make a big difference? Two thousand dollars invested each year at thirteen percent for thirty years will amount to over $650,000. Two thousand dollars invested each year at eight percent will grow to less than $250,000. That's a difference that can't be ignored. The point is that the rate of return and the length of time are the most important variables in the investment equation. They are, surprisingly, even more important than the amount you've invested."

Roy went on, "In the example I just gave you, you would have to invest almost three times as much at eight percent to equal the total earned at thirteen.

"The so-called experts also argue that an investor shouldn't expose his or her retirement savings to even the slightest risk. Their intentions are good, but as I told you in May, properly selected ownership will outperform loaning over the long term — it has to. And what could be more of a long-term investment than an RRSP?" Roy asked rhetorically.

"So we should invest our RRSP money in much the same way we invest our ten percent fund," I concluded.

"Absolutely" was Roy's crisp response. "However, there are a few things you must keep in mind. Tom, real estate is not an eligible RRSP investment. You

couldn't use your RRSP contributions to buy properties with your brother."

"How 'bout with my sister?" Tom kidded.

"Also, as I mentioned earlier, the mutual funds you
purchase must be eighty-two percent Canadian
content in order to conform to government regulations. You cannot buy an international fund unless,
on a cost basis, it represents less than eighteen
percent of the book value of your RRSP. Because the
fund manager's options are limited with a one-coun-
try fund, performance usually suffers slightly. An
RRSP-eligible well-managed equity fund will normally average about three percent less a year than
an equally well-managed international fund. And
because the fund manager's options are limited, it's
more important than ever to select a proven and
capable manager. Use the same techniques we talked
about two months ago and, for heaven's sake, remember the importance of a good long-term track
record." Roy took a sip from his Detroit Tigers coffee
mug. "Any questions?"

"Obviously, we should use a preauthorized chequing plan again," Cathy said in a matter-of-fact tone.

"Yes. To receive the benefits of forced saving and
dollar cost averaging, a PAC plan is the best way to
go." Roy set his mug down and looked at us intently.
"I want to make a very important point here, so listen
carefully. I've cautioned you numerous times that
mutual funds are long-term investments. Over an
extended period, say, a decade, the economy, and
thus the stock market, will normally perform quite
well. Over any short-term period, say, five years or
less, it becomes much more difficult to predict performance with any degree of confidence."

"But we're buying our RRSPs for thirty years, so
who cares?" I shrugged.

"You will care, Dave. . . . All of you will. Let's say
you're fifty years old and you're fairly certain you're

going to retire at age fifty-five. If your RRSP is invested in mutual funds, you're suddenly looking at only a five-year time frame. What if the market performs poorly over those five years? Because you need your RRSP proceeds to augment your income on retirement, you won't have the luxury of being patient. You know Murphy's Law? Well, don't be its victim," Roy warned us.

"If I'm reading you right," Tom hypothesized, "you're saying that as we near our retirement, we should transfer our RRSP funds from ownership — that is, mutual funds — to guaranteed vehicles."

"That's what I'm saying, Tom. Retirement is a long way away for you three now, but promise me that you'll keep this advice in mind. I recommend that when you are within seven or eight years of retirement, you cash out your mutual funds at an appropriate time and purchase guaranteed investments."

"What if seven or eight years before my planned retirement the stock market, and my funds, are at a low point?" Tom inquired.

"That's why I emphasize the words *within* and *at an appropriate time*. Once you're within eight years of retirement, cash out the funds when their value is high — when the markets are strong." Clearly, Roy was impressed by Tom's steady flow of insightful questions. "We'll talk a bit more about timing in the lesson on investing."

"Did you mean cashing out the mutual funds in just our RRSP, or in our RRSP and our ten percent fund?" I wondered.

"Just the RRSP, because that money is needed on a specific date for a specific reason — income creation. The ten percent fund can be held through good times and bad. Even with the RRSP equity funds, you often needn't cash out totally — instead, cash out only the portion you're going to need to have available in a few years."

"Should we avoid common stocks again?"

"Definitely." James Murray put his paper down purposefully. "I'm not in total agreement with Roy. I'm not convinced that all your RRSP money should be invested in ownership. But whatever portion is, it should be managed by a professional, not by a salesperson."

"How do you invest your RRSP money, James?" Cathy asked to humour him.

"Well, I do agree that the odds favour a monthly purchase plan of mutual funds outperforming guaranteed vehicles, but despite that, I still put the majority of my RRSP dollars into guaranteed investments."

Cathy's brow furrowed. "Those two sentences are somewhat contradictory, aren't they?"

"Somewhat, perhaps . . . but not entirely. I own a number of properties. I also own a lot of shares in an international mutual fund. I buy guaranteed products in my RRSP because I feel it makes a great deal of sense to diversify. If the real estate and stock markets go down, at least my guaranteed RRSP investments keep chugging along."

"Is your entire RRSP portfolio guaranteed?"

"No. I have a system. If the stock market has gone down for the two preceding years, I buy a mutual fund with that year's contribution. Buy low . . . you know. If not, I buy guaranteed. Over the years my RRSP has averaged almost eleven percent a year."

"Roy has averaged thirteen percent," Tom one-upped James Murray.

"I rest my case." Roy laughed. "Over the long run, well-selected ownership will always win out. But if you do insist on owning guaranteed products, your RRSP is definitely the place to do it. With no tax being levied on the accumulating interest, even a guaranteed investment will perform well over the years. Plus, you may want to base your decision each year on current interest rates and market conditions, as James does with this 'two-year rule.' Obviously, if rates are at twelve, thirteen, fourteen, or higher, it becomes pretty hard to turn them down."

"You mentioned you could hold your own mortgage in an RRSP. That sounds like a great idea!" I exclaimed.

"It sounds great, but it's not," Roy commented. "If you obtained a $50,000 mortgage from your bank, right now it would probably cost you around $550 a month. If you got a $50,000 mortgage from your RRSP, it would also cost you around $550 a month. You see, under government guidelines, you have to pay the market rate even if you borrow the money from your own RRSP. So it hasn't lowered your monthly costs at all."

"But at least you're paying the interest on the mortgage to yourself," I rejoined, sure that I had made a good point.

"You're not paying it to yourself. You're paying it to your RRSP," Roy rebutted. "And your RRSP is capable of earning interest whether you borrow from it or not. You could buy a guaranteed investment certificate, a GIC, with your RRSP proceeds and earn interest. The only — "

"Yeah, but GICs pay around two percent less than a mortgage costs. So wouldn't your RRSP earn more if you were paying it a mortgage rate instead of it earning a GIC rate?" I persevered.

"Dave, what you say sounds correct, but there is one problem. When you get a mortgage from your own RRSP, there are a number of fees. If you are borrowing less than $30,000 from your RRSP, you will normally end up being worse off than if you had invested the RRSP in GICs — the fees are that substantial."

"So we should only get mortgages from our RRSPs if we're talking more than $30,000," I summarized.

"No. Never get a mortgage from your RRSP because it's — " Roy began.

"Because it's not ownership," Tom, the pecuniary prodigy, finished, as a delighted Roy patted him on the back.

"I disagree again," James Murray leapt in. "I think holding your mortgage in your RRSP makes good sense for substantial RRSP accounts that want to invest conservatively."

"You know, Roy, despite all your knowledge and all your logic, I think I might invest my RRSP primarily in guaranteed vehicles. Like James said, it makes sense from a diversification standpoint and from a tax standpoint. Moreover, I think I'll sleep better knowing my RRSP isn't subject to any risk. I don't have a pension, so my RRSP is paramount." Cathy stated.

With all we had learned from Roy, Cathy's decision seemed like heresy to me.

"I respect your opinion, Cathy," Roy said sincerely. "Your reference to sleeping better is well taken, because you should be comfortable with the investments you make. Even though I am a great advocate of ownership, I have to admit that if there's one place a loaner can succeed — indeed, prosper — it's in an RRSP."

Tom watched approvingly as the final touches were made to his haircut. "Where should we buy our RRSPs, Roy?"

"Mutual fund RRSPs can be purchased from stockbrokers, life insurance agents, and mutual fund salespeople. In addition, many banks and trust companies offer RRSP-eligible funds. But don't forget — not all fund managers are created equal. Do your homework!

"If you choose guaranteed vehicles, as Cathy has and as you two eventually will, I believe you're best to use a *self-administered* RRSP — the type available through brokerage firms and some banks and trust companies.

"First, what is a self-administered RRSP? And second, I thought you labelled brokers poor sources of advice," Tom accused him.

"Whoa now, Tom!" Roy defended himself. "You're misquoting me. I did say not to buy stocks from brokers. But I also said that there are a lot of fine brokers and that they can be a big help in achieving financial success. As it happens, they're one of the best sources of advice on mutual funds. They're also well qualified to assist you in managing your self-administered RRSP.

"And that, to answer your other question, is just what the name implies — an RRSP where you make all the investment decisions. It's like an umbrella, in that one plan can cover all your different investments. Mutual funds, GICs, Canada Savings Bonds, Treasury Bills and even cash can all be housed in the same self-administered plan. Instead of the inconvenience of having plans spread out at ten different institutions, all your registered money is kept in one plan, at one place.

"Unfortunately, most people are scared off by the term *self-administered*. They associate it with stock trading. They don't feel qualified to administer their own plans, anyway. Self-admins were originally designed for the individual who wanted to buy and sell stocks within his or her RRSP. But they're actually perfect for the person who wants to buy guaranteed products . . . And as for going it alone . . . no way. You're not. You can have a trusted and capable broker at your side at all times.

"There are two major factors that make a self-administered plan perfect for the person who wants guaranteed investments. One: it's the only product that can house the full range of guaranteed vehicles — GICs, T Bills, CSBs, bonds, cash . . . the works.

You're not confined to your local bank's limited repertoire . . . GICs and a daily savings vehicle, for example.

"Two: your broker can shop the market for the highest rate. If you have $20,000 available and you want to buy a two-year GIC, you don't have to accept the rate your bank is offering. Your broker can shop the market, locate the best rate, and buy the appropriate choice within your plan. By looking around, the broker can often come up with a rate that is a full percentage point higher than that of your own bank. In our example, that would make a difference of $200 a year. Over the years, that really adds up.

"A self-administered plan is the best way to go for the investor who wants to keep his or her money guaranteed. No ifs, ands, or buts about it. The only caveat is that normally a self-admin costs around $100 a year. This amount can be paid outside the RRSP and is tax-deductible. But until your RRSP holdings are worth at least $10,000 to $15,000, the benefits won't warrant the charge."

"Should I buy a GIC with a one-year, two-year, or five-year term?" My sister was beginning to bear an uncanny resemblance to Diane Sawyer. "Where are interest rates going? Up or down?"

"I have no idea, and neither does anybody else" was Roy's honest reply. "And don't let anyone tell you that he does."

"Or that she does," Tom laughingly directed at the Richardson family feminist.

"No, a woman may be able to . . . use intuition and all that stuff," James Murray deadpanned.

"I want to cover three more points before I let you go," Roy proceeded. "One: if you're married, always name your spouse as the beneficiary of your RRSP. If you don't, the RRSP will normally be included as income on your tax return in the year of your death. If you do, the RRSP can be transferred, tax-free, to

your spouse's name, where it will remain untaxed
until he or she deregisters the plan.

"Two: *spousal* RRSPs. These are little gems. A
spousal RRSP is an RRSP in the name of one spouse,
but whose contributions have come from the other
spouse. Let's use Dave as an example. He puts
$1,000 in an RRSP in Sue's name, thereby creating
a spousal RRSP. He still gets the tax write-off of
$1,000 in the current year, but when the funds are
withdrawn, they are taxed in Sue's name. For people
like Dave, this is a welcome opportunity to save tax
dollars. He gets the deduction now, when he is in a
higher tax bracket than Sue is. She pays the tax on
withdrawal in retirement, when she is presumably
still in a lower tax bracket than Dave, who is receiving a substantial pension. To prevent the abuse of
this generous government offer, though, there is one
special rule. Any monies withdrawn from a spousal
RRSP are taxed in the hands of the *contributor* if any
contribution has been made to the plan in the preceding three years.

"Three: strangely enough, there are two occa-
sions when it may not make sense to contribute to
an RRSP. The first occurs when someone is faced
with the choice of making an RRSP contribution or
financing his or her own business. It's imperative
to plan for retirement but it's even more imperative,
if there is such a term, to put bread on the table
now. If you're starting your own business, it may
mean foregoing an RRSP contribution. Fortunately, with the carry-forward provision, you may
have a second opportunity to contribute. That situation doesn't apply to any of you now, but who
knows . . . someday, Tom might open a dating
service."

"I predict a same-day closing," Cathy noted, gig-
gling.

"The second situation where it makes little sense

to contribute to an RRSP occurs when someone knows there is no chance that he or she is going to need the money later in life. For example, if you are certain that you're going to inherit millions of dollars at some point, why sacrifice your standard of living now to save for what is already guaranteed to be a prosperous retirement?"

"I don't think any one of us is in that boat," Cathy lamented, while my mind drifted to the fact that, as an only child, Sue does stand to inherit a rather large sum of money from her parents one day. Still, you shouldn't plan around inheritances, only enjoy them. I'll be making RRSP contributions as long as the limits allow.

"What if someone can afford only to make an RRSP contribution or to save ten percent?" Tom asked Roy.

"Again, try for both, but if you can come up with the money for only one, go with the RRSP because of the tax incentives.

"My parting comment," Roy said with pleasure, "is that you three have come a long way. You're asking intelligent questions. You're applying what you're learning. You're on your way to becoming very wealthy. Congratulations!"

Cathy acted as our spokesperson. "We owe it all to you, Roy. We can't thank you enough."

"Well, as a matter of fact, you can," Roy informed us, as we paid for our haircuts. "Give me your tickets for tomorrow's Tiger game."

"No way!" Tom roared. "Nothing's worth that much! But you'll be our first guest when we get season's tickets ten years from now."

|7|
HOME,
SWEET HOME

"Well, if it isn't Jack Nicklaus," Jimmy bellowed, as I entered Roy's with Cathy and Tom. "When did they add Sarnia to the tour?"

"The Golden Bear! This is such an honour! Can I have your autograph?" James Murray gushed. "It's for my wife, of course!"

"Did you win a trophy or something?" Roy wondered.

"Slow down, guys," I replied. "I feel like I'm on 'Meet the Press.' No, Sarnia's still not on the circuit. Yes, you can have my autograph. And yes, Roy, I won a trophy."

"What club did you hit?" asked Clyde, offering me a doughnut.

"Yes, let's relive the whole event," Tom cut in sarcastically. "Hey, I've only heard the details 200 times. . . . It's a sunny, windless Tuesday afternoon as Dave Richardson steps up to the third tee. One hundred and sixty yards stretch before him. Water lies on the left. A bunker lurks on the right. Perils abound. Dave laughs in the face of danger, pulls out a seven iron, takes a smooth, sweet swing and . . . the ball rockets straight ahead . . . takes one small skip . . . and lands right in the hole.

"The crowd — consisting of Mr. Richardson and me — goes crazy. So does Dave. He doesn't just get a hole-in-one. Oh, no. He also gets a career-low score of seventy-three. And in the process he takes his closest and most loyal friend, as well as his own flesh and blood, for every cent they have. Of course, we made him buy us and everyone else in the clubhouse a drink. History was made that fateful afternoon. It was an honour to be a part of it, in my own small, humble way."

"Jealousy rears its ugly head," I laughed.

"When are you heading back to Kitchener, Jack? For that matter, when's Mrs. Nicklaus due?" Roy inquired.

"We leave Monday. I can't believe that five weeks have come and gone," I answered, shaking my head. "Sue's due in sixteen days — September fifth, to be exact."

"You must be getting pretty excited."

"*Excited* is not the word. I can hardly sleep at night. Not only are we about to have a baby, but we're also going to buy a house sometime in the next month or so. Parenthood, home ownership, and a Tiger drive to the pennant, all in one month. Unbelievable!

"You know, it's funny. I'm more nervous about buying a house than I am about being a father. How hard can changing diapers be? It's the thought of borrowing $80,000 that makes me a little queasy."

"C'mon, Dave. People say buying a house is the smartest thing they've ever done . . . the best investment of their lives," Tom consoled me.

"You'll never regret buying a house, Dave. I'll guarantee it," James Murray affirmed confidently.

"It's true," Cathy agreed. "You know what they say, 'Renting is like throwing your money away.'"

"What a coincidence! Home ownership is today's subject. Actually, it's not such a coincidence," Roy admitted. "I was going to discuss saving and the use of credit, but I don't see any harm in delaying that until next month.

"Let me start by saying that whoever the ubiquitous 'they' are who say 'renting is like throwing your money away' aren't accurate. I've read that opinion in several well-known financial planning guides, and I just don't know where the authors are coming from. Paying rent is no more throwing your money away than is buying food or clothing. You need shelter. It's one of the three basic necessities of life. Renting is one way to acquire that shelter, and in some cases, it's a very intelligent way.

"I'll let you in on another secret. The reason that the vast majority of homeowners say that their house is the best investment that they've ever made is simple — it's usually the only investment that they've ever made. My customers are always saying to me, 'Yep, Roy, my house is the best investment the wife and I have ever made.' I ask them, 'What else have you invested in?' 'Hmm,' they reply, 'we bought some old stamps one time . . . oh, and a stock on the Alberta exchange.' I'm sure you get my drift. The fact — "

"Hold on, Roy," I interrupted. "You're not trying to tell us that you don't believe in home ownership, are you? I've never heard of anyone who lost money through home ownership. And you get to live there rent-free, too."

"No, Dave, I'm not saying that I don't believe in home ownership. But I am saying that there are some widely held misconceptions about the investment merits of owning a home. Do I believe you should own a home, Dave? Yes. But do I believe everyone should own a home? No!

"As I said a moment ago, along with food and clothing, shelter is one of life's three *essentials*. Everyone needs shelter and it can be obtained in only two ways — you can rent it or you can own it."

"I want to own," I interjected emphatically. "Mom and Dad bought our house thirty years ago for

$15,000. Today it's worth over a quarter of a million. That's phenomenal!"

"What rate of return does that represent?" Roy asked me.

"I don't know. It's grown over fifteen-fold in thirty years. It must be a pretty high rate of return," I reasoned.

"Ten percent, almost exactly. A ten percent average annual compound rate of return. Is that phenomenal?" Roy questioned.

"No, I suppose not. But they also got to live there rent-free all those years," I pointed out.

"Now you're getting to the heart of the matter, Dave. How much of a down payment did your parents make?"

"I remember Dad telling me that they put down twenty-five percent, so that's . . . "

"It's $3,750," Tom responded quickly, rescuing me.

"Leaving them a mortgage of $11,250. The monthly payment on that mortgage would have been approximately equal to what it would have cost them to rent a similar home," stated Roy.

"So in reality," he continued, "they didn't turn $15,000 into a quarter of a million. They turned $3,750 into a quarter of a million."

"You've lost me," Cathy confessed, shaking her head.

"Your parents only invested $3,750 of their own money. The rest was borrowed. And though they obviously had to pay the money back, the costs of doing so were roughly equal to what their rent would have been had they been tenants in the same house — meaning that buying the house really only cost them the down payment. Their monthly mortgage cost was not much different from what their rent would have been.

"Look at Tom's real estate deal. The place cost $77,000, with the mortgage being for $57,000. The monthly mortgage payment, including taxes, is about $670. That amount is being covered by the rent. Therefore, Tom and his brother's only cost is the down payment.

"Your own home is really no different, except you are your own tenant. Your mortgage costs are being covered by your own rent . . . rent you would have had to pay, anyway," Roy concluded.

"You're saying that our parents didn't turn $15,000 into $250,000; they turned $3,750 into $250,000. Right?" I repeated Roy's earlier statements to confirm my understanding.

"Precisely, Dave," Roy agreed. "And that represents an average annual compound return of . . . almost exactly fifteen percent." Roy's answer was aided by James Murray's trusty watch calculator.

"Is that all?" queried Cathy.

"Is that all?" Roy echoed, with a look of dismay.

"I didn't mean it that way," Cathy defended herself. "I realize fifteen percent is a great rate of return. It's just that I thought it would take a lot more than a fifteen percent return to turn $3,750 and change into a quarter of a million over thirty years."

"The magic of compound interest never ceases to amaze," Jimmy said absent-mindedly, as he gazed at August's centrefold. Seeing us staring at him, he blushed and muttered, "Interesting article."

"That's a fantastic rate of return, Roy," Tom resumed, after looking over Jimmy's shoulder appreciatively. "Especially since it's tax-free, isn't it? And the whole time that you're making all that money, you get to enjoy living in the comfort of your own home. No wonder people say their house is the best investment they've ever made!"

"Your points are well taken, Tom," Roy began. "Your principal residence, that is, the home you own and in which you live, can be sold without triggering any tax liability."

"Could my wife and I each own a house and — "

"Nice try, Dave, but no. Since 1981, each family is allowed only one principal residence at a time."

"I guess my property doesn't qualify," Tom surmised.

"That's right, because you don't live in it," Roy concurred.

"The tax-free status of your principal residence when you sell it does indeed make it an appealing investment. That benefit, combined with real estate's finest quality — _leveragibility_ — makes owning your own home unbeatable," James Murray stated in a very matter-of-fact tone.

"Leveragibility?" Cathy and I said simultaneously.

"That's an investment term coined by one of the finest financial minds of our time — me. Leveragibility applies to an investment that has not only the ability to be leveraged, that is, to be borrowed against, but also has the ability to produce an income to offset the costs of being leveraged. You see, not only can you borrow against the value of your real estate property, that is, mortgage it, you can usually cover the costs of that borrowing from the rental income. It's that leveragibility that makes real estate the greatest investment of all time," replied a very convincing James Murray.

"I really think you should be on late-night TV flogging seminar kits, James," Roy said in amusement. "I do agree that leveragibility, as you call it, is the reason that real estate is such an attractive investment. As I showed with our earlier examples, the fact that rental income can offset borrowing costs means that a relatively small investment, the down payment, can grow dramatically even if real estate values only grow by ten percent a year . . . or even if they grow by less than that."

"If you had purchased a house in Kitchener a few years ago, Dave, for $100,000, today it might be worth $125,000 — up twenty-five percent. But remember, you only put $25,000 down, so that $25,000 increase in your home value represents 100 percent return on your investment. Your mortgage payments are covered by the rent — whether it's you paying the rent or a tenant."

It's not hard to see why James Murray does so well in business. He believes in what he's selling.

"Leveragibility, tax-free status on sale, and the joys of owning your own home — why would anybody rent? Here's an even better question: why am I renting?" Tom wondered aloud.

"Despite everything we've said, there are some legitimate reasons for renting, Tom," Roy assured him. "For some people, it may well be better to rent than to own.

"There was one iffy assumption in our previous examples, but none of you picked up on it. When I was speaking of your parents' monthly mortgage payment, I said that it would have been approximately the same as the cost to rent a similar home. James and I maintained that assumption of equality between a mortgage payment and rent throughout our other examples. The prob — "

"I see it," Tom leapt in. "I definitely see it! You've assumed that the place you choose to rent will be similar to the residence you choose not to buy. That may not be the case. In fact, it rarely is the case. Look at me. I'm not about to rent a two-bedroom house. My apartment is more than sufficient."

"You seem to be developing an excellent financial mind, Tom," Roy said sincerely. "Do you two understand the significance of his comment? For a lot of individuals, the assumption that a potential mortgage payment will equal their cost in rent is a false one. Tom's case epitomizes the situation in which many single people find themselves. They're looking at rent of $450 or a mortgage payment of $850. Suddenly, *renting versus buying* is no longer *apples versus apples*. Yes, home ownership still provides a solid investment vehicle fueled by leveragibility and a preferential tax treatment. But it is also going to cost $400 a month more than renting. That's a lot of money. What if Tom rented all his life and added that $400 difference to his ten percent fund? How do you think he would fare?"

Roy's point was a good one. The three of us were now fully aware of the power of compound interest.

"It seems to me that many single people today are desperate to become homeowners. This compulsion is the result of two things; one: parents are telling even their unmarried children that buying a house is the smartest thing that anyone could ever do; two: the cost of houses has risen so dramatically during the eighties that many people fear that if they don't buy now, they'll never be able to. This panic is unwarranted. There are far worse things than renting your shelter."

"The hole I see in your argument, Roy, is that you are assuming people will invest the difference between the cost of buying and the cost of renting. Most won't," James Murray charged.

"I'll grant you that home ownership is the ultimate forced-savings program, and that's one of its other big benefits," Roy conceded. "You have to make your mortgage payment or the bank tends to get annoyed. But I believe that through paying oneself first, a renter can discipline him or herself to save some of the difference in cost between owning and renting. I say *some* because it's not necessary to save the entire difference to come out ahead."

"Why do you say that?"

"Look at the homeowner for a second. He or she is thrilled that his or her — "

"Its?" I suggested helpfully.

"Good idea, Dave. 'Its' home value is rising, but in most cases, that increased value does 'it' little good. If 'it' wants to move, all the other houses in 'its' area are up in price, as well. And — "

"Enough of this 'it' pronoun," Cathy protested. "'It' really doesn't apply to anyone except Tom."

"True." James Murray smiled, then added, "So what if the homeowner wants to sell and then rent? Then the rise in value has helped him."

"Yes, admittedly then it has. But you know something funny? That seldom happens. Aging adults who voluntarily sell and then move to an apartment or old folks' home are few and far between. In most instances, people die still owning their home. So in a way, they haven't benefited from their homes' increased value."

Roy's argument was valid. Of Sue's and my eight grandparents, six had died homeowners. And even though my surviving grandmother, the devoted Blue Jays fan, now lives at Heaven's Gate, she still owns her old home.

"We're not in total agreement here, Roy." This was no surprise, coming from James Murray. "I've known several people who have sold their homes and used the proceeds to augment their retirement income. In addition, the people who haven't sold live rent-free now."

"True," acknowledged Roy, "but I would argue that the real costs of home ownership, even without a mortgage, come close to the cost of renting an adequate apartment. Property tax, insurance, utilities, hydro, upkeep, and let us not forget time, add up to a hefty annual cost.

"I don't want to belabour this point. I do think home ownership is an excellent investment . . . one of the best. But *excellent* and *perfect* are not synonymous. I just want to inform our young friends here, especially the single ones, that renting is not throwing your money away. Look at Clyde, that slothful soul. He's rented all his life, and because his monthly costs to rent are substantially less than his costs would be to own, he's been able to spend more on other things, *and* he's been able to save more than ten percent of his income."

"Even though I do believe in real estate, I'm happy to hear you say all this, Roy," Tom admitted. "The investment merits of home ownership appeal to me, but I hate fixing things, cutting the lawn, wallpapering, and all that domestic junk. Plus, if I bought even a small house on my salary, I'd definitely feel the pinch. I could do it, but I wouldn't have much money left over for travelling and golfing . . . and girls."

"Yeah, your fantasy life is pretty rich," Cathy teased.

"There you go," Roy said to James Murray triumphantly. "A perfect example of someone who is better off renting. Don't worry, though, James. Now he'll have more money to buy bargain properties with his brother, so you'll still make money from him."

"It may interest you to know, Roy, that with half of my commission from Tom's deal, I had their driveway repaved." James Murray had bristled.

"It's true, Roy," Tom said in a kind manner. "I don't mean to blow his cover, but James Murray is a generous guy."

"Boy, James, I bought my condo from you, and you didn't even take me out for lunch," Cathy complained with a wink.

"Speaking of your condo, Cathy, there's an example of a sound investment decision." Roy's compliment seemed to surprise my sister. "With your income and your expensive tastes, I'm sure you wanted a nice place overlooking one of the two marinas. Am I right?"

"Yes," Cathy replied sheepishly.

"Well, there's a perfect example of a case where it was better to buy. I'm sure your mortgage costs and condo fees are about the same as the rental costs for a comparable location."

"Almost exactly the same. That's why I decided to buy." Cathy shrugged. "I figured I might as well be an owner if the costs weren't any different."

"Well, they were a little different in that by buying you gave up the use of your down payment. But nonetheless you did make the right move. Plus, you bought a condo, so you won't have to be involved in maintenance and repairs — "

"I just don't have time for that, Roy," Cathy agreed.

"Dave, you seem to be heading in the right direction, too. With a child on the way and Sue working out of the home, you'll need the space a house provides. Ownership is probably a good move," Roy concluded, as he brushed off my shirt.

"*Probably* is not the word I want to hear, Roy." I frowned, as I abdicated the barber chair to Tom.

"I say probably because there is one time when even the individual to whom home ownership seems ideally suited is best advised not to buy."

"Now there's a contradictory sentence," I noted.

"No, Dave, that situation can exist. Just ask the folks in Calgary. If home prices are about to drop, obviously one is best not to buy," responded Roy.

"Yeah, obviously," I consented. "But Calgary was different. It's basically a one-industry town. When oil went down, so did the town. Kitchener, on the other hand, is the most diversified community I know of. Certainly in areas not dominated by one industry, we don't have to worry about real estate ever declining much."

"You're wrong. Real estate can go down. In most areas, real estate has been on a steady climb since the depression, but no trend lasts forever," Roy cautioned.

"Roy, I respect your opinion, and I realize you know a tremendous amount about financial matters, but nobody I read thinks real estate is going to go down," Cathy argued. "They're not making any more land."

"The famous *finite-land* argument." Roy smiled. "Yes, there is a finite amount of land, albeit that it works out to hundreds of acres per capita in Canada.

"Look, I'm not saying real estate is definitely going to go down. But I do want to alert you to that possibility.

"Over the past several years, a few factors have combined to cause the prices of homes in many areas to skyrocket. Women have entered the work force in unprecedented numbers. Canadians are having fewer children. Both of these developments result in higher disposable family incomes. Much of that higher disposable income is being spent on housing. In addition, the baby boom generation has matured and is fueling an increase in the demand for housing. And on top of all that, people are no longer averse to borrowing heavily. In fact, over the past fifty years borrowing has gone from a shameful vice to the national pastime. Instant gratification is our society's modus operandi. The consumer-debt rate is alarming. These trends can't continue forever. Demographics don't support real estate prices to the same level they have in the past twenty years."

"Roy, why the hell didn't you tell me this before I closed my deal?" Tom demanded intensely.

"For a number of reasons, Tom. One: as Cathy pointed out, several experts don't share my somewhat pessimistic view. Two: I don't think real estate is going to collapse. I do believe, however, that it may post lower average returns. It's still a fine, fine, long-term investment. Three: you bought an undervalued property in an area that has not been subject to the tremendous run-up in prices. Four: you bought near water. I know that sounds funny, but it's a fact of real estate investing that property near water seldom loses its value. Five: your brother is capable of increasing the value of the place handsomely with little expense. Last: you fixed your mortgage costs for five years and your rental income for three. All in all, I think you're in fine shape even if we do see tough times.

"The people who I think should be worried or at least careful are the ones who have a lot of heavily leveraged property without a lot of other assets backing them up."

"What about me, Roy? Would you suggest I wait to buy?" I questioned eagerly.

"No, Dave. As I said earlier, with the baby about to arrive and Sue working at home, it would be nice for you to own a house. You're in a fine city. You don't have to worry about losing your job, and you've got a healthy down payment. Besides —"

"Roy could be dead wrong," James Murray interrupted.

"True," Roy said with a wide grin.

"This is how I feel about home ownership," he continued, after reflecting for a moment. "For most people, it's an excellent investment. Leveragibility, tax-free gains, forced saving, pride in ownership, and reading the paper by the fireplace make it pretty tough to beat. My house is more than just a good investment. It's also my most prized possession. All I've been trying to do is warn you that it's not always best for everyone to own. But I should add before James does that even if you bought for the wrong reasons and at the wrong time, you would probably still fare pretty well over the years."

James Murray rose and applauded.

"Can you give me some tips on buying, Roy?" I moved on. "What should I look for?"

"When you go to buy a house, you should look at it from two angles — "

"Yeah. The front and the back," Clyde quipped.

"Good one, Clyde" was Roy's sarcastic rejoinder. "The house should fit your needs and wants, _and_ it should also fill the requirements of a good investment. No one can tell you what suits your needs and wants except yourself — "

"And his wife," roared Clyde.

"And his wife" — Roy chuckled — "but I can give you some tips with regard to the investment side of things.

"The age-old adage about buying the worst house on a nice street and fixing it up still holds. Location remains the key to buying any real estate, including a home. Proximity to schools, public transportation, and shopping is important.

"You want to make sure that as other homes rise in value yours rises proportionately, at the least. To do this, you must make sure that potential buyers will always find your house attractive. The more potential buyers who feel that way, the better. Build a deck; people love decks. You'll get back your money and more. Buy a home with a fireplace; people love fireplaces. Minor cosmetic surgery will pay for itself many times over. Strictly from an investment standpoint, I advise you against a pool. Most people don't want one. So when you go to sell, there will be fewer potential buyers — less demand. Less demand translates into a lower selling price."

"Yeah, but I'm one of the few who does want a pool."

"Then get one. When it comes to home ownership, it's more important to fulfill your needs and wants than to make the perfect investment. You have to live there every day."

Roy paused to look at a striking blonde passing the window. "My niece," he claimed.

"That's it?" I fretted. "No more tips?"

"Hey, buy the house you and Sue like. Assuming, of course, that you can afford it. I can't tell you what house to buy. Our tastes are a lot different. I like a shag rug on my bedroom floor; you like a mirror on the bedroom ceiling — "

"I've got one of those, too, Dave!" Jimmy crowed.

"I don't have a mirror on the bedroom ceiling, Jimmy. You're weird." A change of subject was definitely in order. "What mortgage and amortization terms should I take, Roy?"

"Do you three have a full understanding of the difference between a mortgage term and an amortization term? The mortgage term is how long the mortgage agreement is binding. Among other things, the mortgage agreement sets out the interest rate, the method of payment, the penalty clauses, and the pay-down options. The amortization term is the length of time over which the debt is to be fully paid off.

"If you borrowed $50,000 to buy a home, taking out a five-year mortgage at twelve percent and selecting a twenty-five-year amortization term, it would cost you $516 a month." Roy must have relied on memory for this example, as he didn't even check with James Murray.

"For twenty-five years?"

"No, for five years. Then the mortgage term would expire. At that time, if interest rates had remained unchanged, you would continue to pay $516 a month, and you would have twenty years left to eliminate the debt. However, if interest rates had risen to fourteen percent, you would have to adjust your monthly payments accordingly. Make sure when you renew your mortgage that you don't select a twenty-five-year amortization again. You'll never pay off your loan! You must adjust your amortization period downward by at least the length of the expiring mortgage term each time your mortgage term expires. Sorry, that was a little wordy," Roy apologized.

"I have very strong convictions about what mortgage and amortization terms most people should select," he resumed. Cathy, whose one-year mortgage term was about to expire, was paying close attention. "Nobody, and I mean nobody, can accurately predict the future course of short-term or long-term interest rates. There's one guy in the States who is paid hundreds of thousands of dollars a year to consistently forecast interest rates incorrectly. Just think what he would make if he were consistently right! Because no one can predict the future, it's very difficult to decide what mortgage term to take. 'What if I take a one-year term and rates rise to eighteen percent? I'll be in big trouble.' 'What if I take a five-year term and rates go down to six percent? I will have wasted all that money.' It's a tough call.

"But James and I do agree on this point: in most cases, a five-year term is the way to go. If you know you can afford to make payments based on the five-year rate, you'll never be in trouble. Basically, you're fixing your costs, and in most cases you can be sure your income will be rising. Sure, sometimes rates will go down and you'll wish you had selected a shorter term. But sometimes they'll go up and you'll be thankful you're protected by a five-year term. It comes down to risk versus reward. The risk is that rates may fall, and you'll be paying more than your buddies . . . but you will be surviving! The reward is that if rates rise dramatically you'll not be forced to sell your house. You'll have peace of mind — and that cannot be overrated."

"What if rates are already at twenty percent when you go to get your mortgage?"

"Good question. In that case, I would take a short-term mortgage, hoping rates will go down," Roy responded thoughtfully.

"But you said it's impossible to predict rates."

"I also said *hoping*, not *predicting*. If rates rise

substantially above twenty percent for any significant period of time, you'll have bigger problems to worry about than your mortgage . . . like the guys with the guns on your front lawn. Certainly, the level of interest rates at the time you select your mortgage will play a part in your decision, but most of the time, five-year is the way to go."

"I do agree." James Murray watched Roy's "niece" pass by again in the opposite direction. "The guy who takes a six-month term, then a one-year, then a variable-rate, trying the entire time to predict the future, is only kidding himself. Yes, sometimes, in fact a lot of times, things will work out for him. He might well end up better off than his five-year friends. But the one time he doesn't, things could get ugly. Besides, some people, I swear it, lose sleep over the whole thing. They call me up and ask where interest rates are going to be in two months."

"What do you say?"

"I tell them we can't be sure where we'll be in two months, let alone where the interest rates will be," he commented wryly.

I pushed on. "What about the amortization period?"

"I suggest you start with a fifteen-year term. In a way, amortization is the reverse of compound interest. In the early years, your payments are almost all interest. Only slowly, as the years progress, do you start eating away at the outstanding principal. In two months, we're going to talk at length about the merits of paying down your mortgage. For now, suffice it to say that it is a very good idea . . . very good for your financial health. One of the best and easiest ways to do that is to shorten your amortization period," Roy answered.

Tom stared at Roy in the mirror. "Is it affordable?"

"At twelve percent, a $70,000 mortgage, amortized over twenty-five years, costs $722 a month. That same mortgage, amortized over fifteen years, costs $827 a month. An extra $100 a month will save you ten years worth of payments . . . and thousands in interest." Roy set his mortgage tables down beside his Tiger schedule, two invaluable documents if ever there were any.

"And because it's forced saving, it's not that tough to do," Cathy deduced proudly.

"All this forced saving is bound to get a little tough on us sooner or later," I remarked half-seriously.

"We'll talk about saving and credit management next month, Dave. Believe me, you will make it through all this without having to hock your hole-in-one trophy," the wealthy barber assured me.

"A couple of other points about your mortgage," he went on, as he trimmed Tom's sideburns. "One: if it's at all possible, pay weekly. It really does have a major effect on your total payments. Two: shop the market for the best rate. Don't assume your bank is your wisest choice. The one down the road may be offering mortgages at half a percentage point less. That, too, can make a big difference.

"Any questions?"

"I have one. Suppose your job demands that you move every couple of years. Should you buy a house each place you go?"

"Good question, Dave. It has absolutely nothing to do with anyone in this room, but it's a good question, nonetheless," Roy grinned. "Even the staunchest of real estate supporters would agree that, over a one- or two-year term, it's impossible to predict price movements. Keep that in mind. Also keep in mind the fact that some of the cities our imaginary friend is transferred to may be riskier investments because they're one-industry towns. In light of all that, I would advise him to buy a property in his hometown. That's assuming it's a good time to buy and a good city and he can rent his property out while he rents his residence in each of his stops. That way he will be able to take part in real estate's solid long-term growth without being subject to the risks of short-term ownership. A few oil company executives I know who are currently stationed in Sarnia are following that strategy. They rent nice homes here while owning houses back in Toronto. Sometimes they don't even bother to rent out their Toronto homes. I guess they don't need the money."

"They must get their hair cut here, too," kidded Tom. "What about young couples today? If I were to get married and wanted to buy a house, it would be difficult for me to afford a nice one, even with my wife's income. And it's even worse for young couples in places like Toronto."

"Unfortunately, I don't have any brilliant answer for that problem," Roy said with a sigh. "Through proper financial planning, especially through the use of a ten percent fund, it will be possible for any couple to buy a nice home at some point in the future. I stress *at some point*, because it could be several years down the road. If a young couple wants to buy a house soon after getting married, they're going to have to accept the fact that it won't be easy. The high prices of the past several years make saving a sufficient down payment a tough task. It means sacrificing other things — staying in on weekends; not going to Florida; doing without a dishwasher and a microwave and a VCR. It's funny, but only in these days of instant gratification would these sacrifices seem totally unfair. Most of us old fogies sacrificed considerably more in our early years in order to save a down payment — like cars, newspaper subscriptions, and good winter coats.

"There are a couple of possibilities young couples should keep in mind. One is borrowing all or part of the down payment from a relative. Parents and grandparents tend to be a little more flexible when it comes to terms. Usually something can be worked out where everybody is happy. A lot of people borrow their down payment from relatives and pay them a couple of interest points under the going rate. Obviously, this is a good deal for the borrower. Not so obviously, it can also be a good deal for the lender. Why? Because this way, most of the time no tax is paid on the interest; whereas, if it was invested in the bank, it would be subject to tax at the loaner's marginal tax rate."

"Isn't that illegal?" Tom asked, as he rose.

"Yes. I don't think you should do it. I just said there are people doing it. A second possibility young couples should keep in mind is the opportunity to rent out a room of their newly purchased home. Perhaps a friend needs a place and your basement has a bedroom, bath, and kitchenette. Perfect! That extra two or three hundred a month could be what it takes to enable you to buy the property you want.

"It's not easy for young couples to buy a house these days. Yet somehow most of them manage to do it and get by just fine. I don't think this problem is new; I think it's just getting more press now because young people today think that when they leave their parents' nest by some divine right they should move directly into an air-conditioned birdhouse. Ah, if only life were that easy!"

"I hate to admit it, Roy, but you're right about me and my contemporaries. We do tend to have high and often unrealistic expectations. Fortunately, some of us are doing our best to learn how to not only meet those expectations but also to surpass them . . . with your help, of course," I thanked him indirectly.

"Next month?" Tom prompted.

"Saving, spending, and credit management."

"Gee, Cathy could be a guest expert on one of those three," Tom tossed over his shoulder as he rushed into the street in search of Roy's "niece."

|8|
SAVING SAVVY

I entered Roy's to a standing ovation.

"Here he is! The father of the year!" Roy beamed with avuncular pride.

"Samantha?" James Murray tsk'ed, while a painfully tone-deaf Clyde hummed the "Bewitched" theme song. "Were you an Elizabeth Montgomery fan when you were young?"

"You think you're kidding. That's exactly why we chose Samantha," I answered honestly. "Both Sue and I loved that show."

"Hey, guys, I'm expecting my nephew to be named either Darrin or Dr. Bombay," Cathy tossed in. "And does this mean that I have to marry a man named Arthur?"

"Clyde, what's with the black armband?" Tom wondered.

"I'm wearing it out of respect for you, Dave, James, and Roy . . . and out of respect for your dearly departed Tigers, the once-proud ball club that was suddenly, inexplicably, struck down in late August . . . a sad moment indeed," Clyde sympathized, with all the sincerity of a game-show host.

"We'll get 'em next year." My rejoinder was woefully short on conviction.

"Back to a more cheerful topic, Dave," Roy said, to

rescue me from despair. "How are Sue and the baby? Everything went well?"

"Perfectly. Sue was only in labour for three hours. I myself played a major part in the delivery. I told her, 'Breathe in, breathe out — '"

"Good advice," Clyde injected sarcastically.

"To answer your other question, Roy, they're both just great. Sam is beautiful. She takes after her mother, thank God," I added before one of them could.

"Can she wiggle her nose?" wondered Jimmy.

"Everyone's a comedian," I noted.

"And word has it that you bought a house, too. Congratulations!"

"Thanks, Roy. Yeah, it's been quite a month. We bought an older home on a nice quiet street in Kitchener. Hard as it may be to believe, we actually spent about $10,000 less than we had planned to. We took one look at the place and knew it was the house for us. The previous owners had really kept it up well. It has a new roof and a new furnace. The pipes and the wiring were redone just seven years ago. We have a den, a sunroom, and even a gazebo. You guys should come and see it. . . . No, come to think of it, we're busy that weekend."

"All right, let's get started," Roy broke in. "I'm in a real hurry. I have to close up shop by ten-thirty. Marj's niece, Laura, is getting married in London. Yowza." He yawned. "Yep. I'm pretty excited about the whole thing."

"C'mon, Roy. Give and take. I'm sure Marj isn't always thrilled about everything she has to do with you," countered Cathy.

"In my defence, Cathy, I didn't complain at all when I had to go to Laura's first two weddings. But now that her 'sacred' day has become an annual event, Marj's and my nerves are wearing thin . . . as is our pocketbook." This comment drew a laugh from everyone.

"I've got to warn you, Roy," began Tom. "I was saying on the way here that for the first time in half a year I wasn't particularly looking forward to our monthly trip to the barber. Your guidance on how to create wealth has been fantastic, but it's hard to get psyched up about a lecture on the merits of thrift. Don't buy fancy cars; don't abuse credit cards; don't borrow to go on trips; look after the nickels and dimes and the dollars will look after themselves; don't underestimate the power of coupons; a penny sa —"

"We get the point." Roy put an abrupt end to the litany. "But my philosophy on today's subject might surprise you."

"What exactly is today's subject? Tom seems to think he knows, but all you said last month was that we were going to discuss saving, spending, and credit management. So," I ventured, "is what we're really talking about the proper handling of our day-to-day financial affairs?"

"That's not a bad way of putting it," Roy commended me. "In this instance, by *saving*, I mean saving for things like trips, VCRs and cars, not saving as in the ten percent fund and RRSPs. By *spending*, I mean purchasing goods from groceries to large-screen TVs, not investing. And by *credit management*, I mean the use of credit cards, lines of credit, and personal loans, not investment loans and mortgages. So the proper handling of our day-to-day financial affairs is probably a perfect description of today's agenda."

"But Tom probably wasn't far off the mark with his little routine, either," Cathy speculated. "You're going to give us a lecture on the merits of thrift, comparison shopping, and a debt-free net-worth statement."

"I confess that I used to espouse — in fact, *preach* may be a better word — the benefits of those things.

Historically, my lesson on today's subject wasn't unlike Tom's speech at all."

Tom asked the obvious question, "What happened to change that?"

"Nobody listened." Roy's wry chuckles didn't mask the seriousness of his response. "Oh, I shouldn't say nobody. Some of my pupils followed my advice on saving, spending, and credit management. Well, at least one did. And he's certainly not in this room." Roy was directing his remarks at James Murray, Jimmy, and Clyde.

"After all — " Tom began.

"Let me finish," Roy said politely. "Almost everyone I've taught over the years has developed the winning habit of saving ten percent of his or her income and investing it for growth. I would guess that ninety-five percent of them have drafted wills and purchased and maintained appropriate life insurance. They've shortened their amortization periods. They've contributed annually to their RRSPs. Basically, they combined common sense with simple but effective strategies to move towards all their financial goals.

"But when it came to following my advice about day-to-day things like developing household budgets, avoiding credit cards, and exercising a degree of self-control — which is really all thrift is — generally, people ignored me."

"Why?" Cathy huffed. "If it weren't for you, many of those people would have faced bleak financial futures."

"As one who chose to ignore the teachings of a man whom he once called 'his financial saviour,' perhaps James could answer that question."

We all turned our attention to James Murray. He smiled. "Saving ten percent of your income and investing it in a properly selected long-term growth vehicle, making a will, buying the proper amount and type of life insurance, maintaining an RRSP, and shortening your amortization period have three great features in common. First, they're easy to understand. You don't have to be a mathematical genius to grasp the advantages of something like dollar cost averaging. Second, they work. All your financial goals can be achieved through the application of these principles. What's more, they can be achieved without a significant lowering of your current standard of living. Third, and equally important, the guidelines are easy to implement and easy to maintain. So I was moving toward the attainment of all my financial goals, and I didn't have to study the stock market pages for hours a week. I didn't have to phone my broker four times a day. I didn't have to spend every Saturday afternoon reading books on investing. While my net worth continued to grow, I played tennis.

"Then Roy sat me down and explained why I should develop a household budget. He told me to keep track of every dime I spent, to read the newspapers each night and write down the items on special, and to save — never borrow — money to go on a trip. I remember that he said, 'You'll enjoy your vacation more, knowing it's paid for.'

"Even as Roy spoke, I knew there was no way that I was going to follow any of that advice. Drive across town to get chicken on special? Get serious! Develop a budget and keep track of every cent? That's just not my style. Ease of implementation? Uh-uh!"

"Let me take it from here, James," Roy commanded. "A couple of years after I had taught James the basics of sound financial planning, we got together to review his progress. His report card read straight A's. His net-worth statement was impressive and getting more so each day. I commended him, and myself, on a job well done. So imagine my surprise when he admitted that he had not followed any of my advice on the managing of day-to-day financial matters! Then he told me that practically no one else had, either."

Cathy frowned in consternation. "Were you upset?"

"No, not at all. I quickly realized that if anything I should feel a deep sense of satisfaction. My overall financial plan had worked in spite of its users' undisciplined approach to daily saving, spending, and credit management. Then I realized that it's really no concern of mine how someone manages his or her day-to-day finances. People weren't coming to me to be told that they shouldn't eat out more than once a week. They were coming to me to learn how they could eventually afford to eat out every night if they wanted to."

"The fact is," Clyde asserted, "what the hell does it matter how I spend my money if I'm already takin' care of my financial planning?"

"Once again, Clyde, you have articulated my point perfectly," Roy said with a chuckle. "I hate to admit it but Mr. Eloquence here is right. Our ten percent savings, RRSP contributions, insurance premiums, and mortgage payments or rent are coming off the top — that is, not being taken from whatever is left over at the end of the month. So how we spend our discretionary income has astonishingly little impact on our financial future. As long as people are following the rest of our financial planning guidelines, how they handle day-to-day finances can safely be left up to them."

"I've got a question, Roy," I declared. "In April or May you spoke out against budgeting. Now you're saying that in the past you've advocated it. Why?"

"The type of budgeting I touched on in the spring is distinctly different from the budgeting I used to recommend to people like James. Nine times out of ten, budgeting that is done to create a savings fund for the future is a losing proposition. As I pointed out months ago, it's virtually impossible to budget accurately for both needs and wants. Too often through rationalization the wants become needs and the seemingly well-balanced budget goes out the window. The type of budgeting that I was recommending to James and others was a household monthly expense budget — a budget confined strictly to needs. To be honest, I still feel that type of budget can be very useful. It's comparable to the shop budget that has worked so well for me over the years," Roy explained.

"You see " — James Murray took over — "most people, including most financial planners, have it backwards. They develop intricate budgets that cover everything from weekly gas expenses to entertainment costs to saving for retirement. Unfortunately, because most of us lack self-discipline, today's concerns receive the bulk of our financial resources. The hundreds of dollars that were supposed to be there at the end of the month to pay down the mortgage and to start up a retirement fund have shrunk or vanished. 'The damn budget's not working,' people cry. But by following Roy's advice we're taking care of financial planning *first*. We can be capricious with the rest of the money, or we can set aside so much for a trip, so much for a new car, so much for groceries — you know, save the way abnormal people like Roy do. It's really a matter of style. But because you're paying yourself first and using forced-saving techniques, someday you'll be wealthy no matter how you manage your day-to-day finances.

"If a financial planner looked at the way Jimmy, Clyde, and I handle our daily finances, he would probably have a heart attack. We buy groceries at variety stores. We get our gas at full-service stations. We don't pay our credit cards off every month. We join health clubs and don't go. Our day-to-day money management is an embarrassment. But we sure look

pretty *in the big picture.* In fact, our net-worth statements look great. None of us will ever have any real
financial worries," James Murray concluded.

I was skeptical. "You don't condone this behaviour,
do you, Roy?"

"Of course not. Using some discipline and common sense, you can get a lot more out of your money
than these guys do. But I have to agree that despite
their devil-may-care approach to saving, spending,
and credit management, all three of them are in
excellent financial shape," Roy acknowledged.

"The problem is that I'm not going to have enough
money left after all this forced saving to enjoy myself.
I'm going to have to become a miser and a bookkeeper
who budgets as meticulously as you," I said
worriedly.

"Not true, Dave" was Roy's straightforward response. "Not true at all. I realize that implementing
the strategies that we've discussed sounds like a lot,
but let's take a closer look. We're all friends here.
Dave, what's your combined monthly take-home
pay?"

"If Sue's articles continue to sell as well as they
have during the past few months — she's doing well;
she's on a pace to make five or six thousand more
freelancing than we thought she would — our take-
home pay should average about $3,300 a month. As
for us all being friends, I — "

"Thirty-three hundred less ten percent is how
much?" Roy overrode me before answering his own
question. "That's 2,970. How much can you contribute to RRSPs on a monthly basis?"

"This year, with my pension adjustment, I'll be
eligible to contribute about $200 a month to a spou-
sal RRSP. Sue should be allowed at least $150 a
month. So that's $350 from $2,970 . . . that's $2,620
left over. Our life insurance premiums total seventy
dollars a month. That leaves $2,550."

"What's your monthly mortgage payment?"

"We selected a five-year term and a fifteen-year amortization period. Our monthly payment is $827. In case you're wondering, and I'm sure you are, our mortgage is for seventy-something thousand," was my detailed response.

"Why didn't you arrange to make weekly payments, like Roy suggested?" Tom inquired.

"The institution we borrowed from doesn't offer *weekly-pay* mortgages. But it did have both the lowest five-year interest rate and the most flexible pay-down privileges." I revelled in my newly developed ability to answer financial questions intelligently.

"All right, Dave, that leaves you with $1,723," Roy calculated. "What other expenses come to mind?"

"Property tax — $100 a month. Car insurance — the same. The costs of running a home — insurance against fire and theft, heat, hydro, water, cable TV, phone, et cetera, et cetera — average $300 a month. All that adds up to another $500. Hey, we're down to a little over $1,200!" I exclaimed anxiously.

"So what's the problem?" Jimmy asked.

"Twelve hundred doesn't sound like much to me," I retorted, disconcerted. "I've got to pay for groceries and entertainment out of that. Plus, I have to save for a new car and clothes and a vacation . . . It won't be easy," I argued.

"Look, I don't want to steal Roy's thunder by reciting his legendary wrap-up speech two months early, but there are a few points that need to be made," a very serious James Murray stated. "One: $1,200 a month for groceries, entertainment, and car expenses is plenty; two: think about what you're accomplishing here. You're saving ten percent and investing it in a well-selected growth vehicle so that someday the finer things in life will be yours. You're doing an excellent job of ensuring that your retirement will be a happy one. You're ridding yourself much more quickly than most people of your biggest liability and the biggest drain on your monthly cash flow — your mortgage. Your estate planning is properly taken care of. If either you or Sue dies, the other will not suffer great financial hardship. My third point is one that Roy hasn't emphasized. In most cases, the monthly sacrifices associated with implementing your financial plan will stay level or decrease while your income continues to climb. Because your living estate is constantly increasing, your insurance needs will gradually decline. Your mortgage costs are fixed for five years and will be gone in fifteen years — or sooner, if you follow the advice Roy will be giving you next month. Four . . . I forget . . . but I'm sure there is a 'four.'"

"Four" — Roy relieved him — "you've forgotten that your RRSP contributions are tax-deductible. Your cumulative total of $350 a month in RRSP contributions should net you an annual tax rebate of approximately $1,500."

"Yeah, there's that vacation you were wondering 'bout, Dave," mumbled Clyde, while he devoured what had to have been his sixth doughnut.

"Just think, Dave." An animated James Murray leapt to his feet."Without doing anything fancy or risky and without pinching your standard of living much at all, you and Sue are on your way to accomplishing all your financial goals. I don't believe for a minute that living on $1,200 a month after all your major commitments and expenses are met is going to put the squeeze on you. But even if it does, remember that every year your discretionary income is going to climb. And all the while, you'll be sleeping like a baby as your friends toss and turn, wondering and worrying about their finances."

"Now that we've reviewed Dave's family income versus expenses, you can see why I no longer feel that how people handle their day-to-day finances will make or break them. Dave and Sue's saving for financial planning reasons is designed to come off the top, that is, to be drawn automatically from their bank account. So even if they mishandle their discretionary income, things should work out well."

"What if Dave goes out and buys a large-screen TV with a built-in stereo? Or what if Sue becomes a chargeaholic and runs up thousands of dollars on the credit card?" Cathy demanded. "I know that their financial planning is assured through forced saving. But I don't think that means they can do and buy whatever they want."

"Of course it doesn't, Cathy," Roy agreed. "I would consider that to be the 'mishandling of discretionary income.' I would rank that right up there with the couple that earns an annual income of $40,000 and buys a brand-new $15,000 car with no money down. What they've managed to do is drain their monthly cash flow, use borrowed money to buy nondurable goods, and lose thousands of dollars as soon as their 'investment' is driven off the lot. From a financial planning standpoint, that's not smart. Neither, however, is it fatal. Most people, even those I've taught, buy new cars with borrowed money all the time. It may not be smart — but I guess it's fun and, for most, affordable.

"Now, the couple that earns an annual income of $40,000 and buys a brand-new $30,000 car with no money down is just plain foolish. Several people in their twenties and thirties have come to me for financial planning advice. I can't believe the number of young people who want not only to achieve all the goals we've discussed but also to own a beautiful house, a fancy car, and a cottage — *now*! They don't need a financial planner; they need a miracle worker! People must live within their means. That doesn't mean they have to scrimp and save every day of their lives, but it does mean they can't spend with reckless abandon.

"Charles Dickens's Mr. Micawber put it best: 'Annual income twenty pounds, annual expenditure nineteen ninety-six, result happiness. Annual income twenty pounds, annual expenditure twenty pounds ought and six, result misery.'"

Truer words were never spoken.

"I have two more questions, Roy," I admitted apologetically. "One of the goals we spoke of earlier hasn't been covered — the ability to finance our children's postsecondary education."

"We'll discuss that in November, in our miscellaneous lesson," Roy promised. "You know . . . November, the month you three are going to present me with a modest token of your appreciation for all that I've done for you."

"What can we get a man who has everything?" Tom asked half-seriously.

"Good point, Tom. Let's see. I've never been given a tip," joked Roy.

"Speaking of tips, you mentioned that you used to give them on the management of day-to-day finances and preach the virtues of thrift. Can you pass along a few to those of us who do want to make the most of our discretionary money? As everyone knows, it's a job requirement in the teaching profession that you be thrifty — "

"Cheap," Tom corrected me.

"I thought it was also mandatory that as a teacher you marry a teacher. How did you get around that one?" Jimmy snickered.

"I'd be happy to give you some tips." Roy's readiness surprised me, considering his time constraints and his earlier claim that he no longer concerned himself with his pupils' handling of day-to-day money. "It's nice to hear from a person who understands the value of a hard-earned dollar." Roy paused to look smugly at James Murray before returning his attention to me. "I won't design a budget for you or teach you how to haggle, one of my specialties, but I will pass on a few rules of thumb.

"First, a dollar saved is two dollars earned." Roy hadn't just made a statement, he'd made a pronouncement. The shop fell silent.

"Think about the significance of that," he encouraged us, breaking the spell.

"I don't even understand it." Cathy spoke hurriedly, aware of the time. "What do you mean, 'A dollar saved is two dollars earned'?"

"Dave, if you got a two-dollar bonus at work, how much more would you take home?"

"It was Cathy who didn't understand, Roy, not me," I said, to refresh his memory. "I'd take home a little more than a dollar. By the time all my deductions had come off, almost half my bonus would be gone. Taxes, pension contributions, unemployment insurance, Canada Pension Plan, union dues . . . they all add up."

"They sure do," Roy agreed. "A two-dollar raise often translates into only a one-dollar increase in disposable income . . . the same increase that would result from saving a single dollar.

"If by buying at a liquidation sale, Tom saves $200 on the price of a VCR, it amounts to pretty much the same thing as getting a $400 bonus. Many people would work overtime on a holiday weekend to earn a $400 bonus, but those same people can't be bothered to spend three hours comparison shopping. It doesn't make sense! To be called *cheap* is an insult — it implies a mean and petty approach to money. What some people don't realize is that to be called *thrifty* is a compliment — it implies a disciplined, economical and common-sense approach to money. It certainly was a virtue during the depression, when I was young! Food for thought, isn't it?"

Even James Murray, Jimmy, and Clyde, the resident spendthrifts, clearly appreciated Roy's point.

"Credit cards are an anathema to well-managed finances" was Roy's second pronouncement. "We all know that if we don't pay off our debt the month it is incurred, it's subject to exorbitant rates of interest. The rate on credit-card debt is often five or six percentage points higher than on standard consumer loans — so don't carry any! If you can't pay off your balance, borrow from the bank, pay off the credit-card company, and owe the bank the money. Their interest rate will be much lower."

"As long as you pay your cards off promptly, they're a pretty good deal, though, right? One month interest-free plus the convenience." CCC, Credit-Card Cathy, desperately wanted Roy's approval.

She was in for a disappointment. "Actually, no. For most people, they're not a good deal. The convenience that you view as positive can combine with human nature to form a destructive force, especially in the hands of someone who loves to shop. How many times have you bought something with your credit card that you wouldn't have bought if you'd had to pay cash? And isn't it usually something that you know you could live without? Then how many times have you opened your credit-card bill, clutched your throat, and shrieked, 'Five hundred dollars! What the heck did I spend it on?' So the fact is that many people who pay off their balance each month are still hurt by their use of credit cards."

"That's me." Tom shook his head ruefully. "I never paid one red cent in interest to a credit-card company, but I still cut up my cards last year. Plainly stated, I was abusing the privilege."

"I have to give you credit, Tom — no pun intended," Cathy sighed. "I should do the same . . . but I don't want to hurt the Canadian economy." I wasn't sure Sis was kidding.

"Many people 'abuse the privilege,' as our friend here so aptly put it. At least you know yourself well enough to admit it, Tom. Credit cards do offer short-term interest-free financing and convenience, but they are not for the undisciplined," Roy summarized.

"Shouldn't we try to avoid consumer debt altogether, not just credit-card debt?"

"Theoretically, yes. I say 'theoretically' because, in some cases, taking on consumer debt can work to the borrower's advantage. But I'll get back to that in a minute.

"If you see a compact disc player that you simply have to have, what's the best way to save for it?" the wealthy barber continued.

"By paying yourself first," Cathy ventured.

"Yeah, by using forced saving," Tom concurred. "It doesn't really matter whether you're saving for retirement or saving for a compact disc player. The most effective way to do it is by paying yourself first."

"Absolutely correct! So if Dave, for example, wants that player, he should arrange to have so much a month come directly off his pay cheque and go into his account at the teachers' credit union. When he has accumulated enough, he will withdraw the funds and buy the CD player. Tom hit the nail on the head when he said that it doesn't matter whether you're saving for retirement or for a luxury item — pay yourself first! The only difference is how you invest the savings. It doesn't take long to save for a consumer item or a trip. For that reason, you must invest the savings conservatively. Mutual funds, real estate, and stocks are not appropriate vehicles for these savings. They offer too uncertain a short-term return. The money should be placed in a competitive guaranteed investment.

"What I mean by 'competitive' is probably best illustrated by an example. Let's say Cathy is saving up for a car that costs $23,000. After one year, she's saved $10,000 . . . not an impossible feat on her enviable income. She's confident that she'll be able to save $1,000 a month in the second year. How should she invest the $10,000 she's already accumulated? Well, she knows she's not going to need it for a year, so instead of settling for the low rates that savings accounts pay, she should buy a one-year guaranteed investment certificate. She should purchase the GIC from a trust company or bank that is covered by Canada Deposit Insurance and that offers a good rate. Don't settle for whatever rate your own bank is offering — shop the market. What I'm really saying is that investing this type of savings should be governed by one thing — common sense."

"Earlier you said that taking on consumer debt can sometimes work to the borrower's advantage," Tom recalled. "When is that true?"

"Can any of you tell me?" Roy challenged us.

"I can!" Cathy had waited a long time to vindicate her passion for plastic. "Debt is the ultimate forced-saving plan. You have to make your payments or . . . or — "

"Or you're in big trouble," Tom helped out.

"Precisely." Roy smiled. " 'The ultimate forced-saving plan' is an excellent way to phrase it, Cathy. There's no way a spendthrift like James would ever have saved up enough money to buy that beautiful boat of his — he doesn't have the discipline. By borrowing, he forced himself to save . . . after purchase, mind you, but still he had to save. And he could enjoy his acquisition in the meantime." For once, James Murray chose not to disagree or expand on a point.

"I'm not suggesting that every time you want something you go out and borrow the money you need to buy it . . . Cathy," Roy said pointedly. "Sooner or later, you would end up in bankruptcy court. And not only can excessive borrowing tap your cash flow, but it can also cause stress. You'll find sleep comes more easily when you're earning interest than when you're paying it.

"Another thing that bothers me about *borrow-to-buy* is that you miss out on the feeling of satisfaction that comes from saving up to buy something you really want. Today some young adults have *never* experienced that feeling of deferred gratification. They have borrowed to buy literally every major asset they have — from their TVs to their cars to their homes."

"There's a lot of truth in what you're saying, Roy," I chimed in. "Sue and I saved for three years to buy our car outright, and it gave us a tremendous feeling. I honestly think that we enjoy the car more because we know it's fully ours."

"Sure. Because though borrowing does have the advantage of forcing you to save, it also has the disadvantages we named earlier. Live within your means!" Roy cautioned us again, while trimming Tom's bangs at a record "clip."

"I have one question, Roy, and once you've answered it, I promise I'll get these two guys out of your hair."

"It's a deal, Cathy."

"Why did you used to recommend to people that they keep track of every dime they spent? That's a lot of work, and is there really any benefit? I mean, what can you do about money that's already gone?"

"The reason I advocated, and still advocate, keeping a detailed *household financial summary* is that it can be very informative. If you don't believe me, try it. Keep a detailed summary of all of this month's expenditures.

"A couple of years after I took over the barbershop, I borrowed money to buy a new car. When I summarized my expenses at the end of the year, I couldn't believe how much of my income was spent on my vehicle. Financing costs, gas, insurance, upkeep . . . close to a third of my after-tax income hit the road with my car. It was clear that though I could pay all my car-associated expenses, I couldn't truly afford the car I was driving. It required too many other sacrifices. So I sold the car and bought a good second-hand one — or a 'previously owned' one, as they like to say now."

"I've never done a 'household financial summary,' as Roy calls it, and I never will," James Murray remarked with a smirk. "A friend of mine did one, though, and I have to admit he benefited from it. He went into shock when he discovered that, over a twenty-two-business-day period, he had spent $250 on lunches. . . . That could add up to three grand a year! Needless to say, he's occasionally brown-bagging it now," he said, laughing.

True to her word, Cathy began to usher Tom and me towards the door. "Thanks for everything, Roy," we said over our shoulders.

"I was just doing a little personal household financial summary in my mind, as you people babbled on," Tom yelled as Cathy dragged us farther out of Roy's. "And do you know what I spend far too much on? Haircuts! I'm spending far too much on haircuts!"

Roy just waved.

9
INSIGHTS INTO INVESTMENT AND INCOME TAX

"Coffee?" Roy offered us, with a warm smile.

"Hell, I d-d-don't even d-d-drink c-coffee, but I'll have one," Tom replied, teeth chattering. Cathy and I just nodded, shivering and stamping our feet.

"I can't remember a colder day for this time of year. That wind chills you right to the bone. . . . You can see your breath . . . and in your case, Tom, it's not a pretty sight," James Murray quipped, to the great amusement of Clyde.

"What the heck is the temperature?" Cathy grimaced.

"Minus somethin'," Clyde stated authoritatively.

"Hey, Clyde, I didn't realize you studied meteorology at school," Tom said facetiously.

"No, I hate that metric stuff," Clyde fired back. We could only hope that he was kidding.

"Roy, before we get started with today's lesson, I want to tell you that something you said last month had a profound effect on me," Cathy announced.

"You mean it took five months for me to say something that had a profound effect on you?" Roy laughed. "I must be doing something wrong."

"That's not what I meant and you know it. Serious —"

"Let me guess what it was," Tom interrupted. "A dollar saved is two dollars earned."

"You must be psychic!"

"Not psychic — psycho," Jimmy called from the back room.

"That same statement had quite an impact on me, too," Tom explained. "I hadn't thought about it before, but Roy was definitely right. Most of us will do anything to earn a few extra bucks, but very few of us will spend even a couple of hours looking for the best deal on, say, a new set of golf clubs.

"Golf clubs come to mind for a reason. Last week, I headed out to buy a new set of irons. I knew exactly what make and model I wanted, but instead of just walking into the local pro shop and paying whatever was asked, I decided to check around. I found the same set of clubs for $180 less at a different pro shop. Shopping around for only three hours saved me almost $200. Not bad, eh?"

"And remember," I commented, "saving $180 is the same as earning a bonus of $360."

"Well, in my case, not quite," Tom corrected me. "For me, saving $180 is the same as earning a bonus of about $300. But my three-hour comparison shopping effort still *earned* me $100 an hour. It has taken twenty-nine years, but I think I've finally learned the value of being thrifty."

"Thriftiness remains a virtue," Roy summarized.

"What's today's topic, Roy?" Cathy asked eagerly. "I seem to recall that October's lesson was to be on investing."

"Today we're going to cover two distinct areas, the first of which is, indeed, investing. Our second topic is everyone's favourite — income tax." Needless to say, this was greeted by a chorus of boos. "Whoa, my friends, do not boo! We're not just going to discuss income tax, we're going to discuss how to reduce our annual income-tax bills." Naturally, this remark met with a more favourable response.

"Why are we discussing investing and income tax on the same day?" I wondered. "Do they dovetail well from a teaching standpoint?"

"The reason that we're discussing them together is quite complex, but here it is . . . " Roy paused and looked pensive. "In terms of time, they each take approximately one haircut to cover."

"That is deep," Tom deadpanned.

"I don't know much about investing, Roy, but I do know that even a teacher as skilled as you can't cover all the ins and outs of investing during one haircut . . . not even if the client is Rapunzel."

"You're right, Cathy," Roy conceded. "To cover the ins and outs of all the different types of investments in that short a time frame would be impossible. But that's okay, because one of the chief prerequisites of a financial plan is that its successful implementation not be dependent on expert investment management by the *plannee*. Why? Because most of us aren't capable of performing in-depth investment analysis, and what's more, most of us don't even want to become capable!"

"Amen," I interjected.

"Successful investing is elusive. If it weren't, everybody would be shopping on Rodeo Drive. Few have the time it takes to properly analyze different investment alternatives. Those who do have the time to assess the risks and rewards of a given investment must also have both strong mathematical ability and sufficient knowledge to enable them to apply that ability wisely. That might involve anything from having an accounting background when studying stocks to having a feel for the local economy when selecting a commercial real estate site."

"I'm sorry to interrupt you here, Roy," apologized

James Murray. "But I want to reiterate something I said way back in May. Not only does successful investing take a lot of time and specialized knowledge, but it also takes tremendous discipline and an eye for value . . . an eye that is often more intuitive than informed."

"I would go one step further, James, and say that without discipline and an eye for value, an investor is doomed to dismal failure. I know several well-trained, well-informed investors who consistently lose money. They lack either the required discipline or the eye for value. Conversely, I know people who lack specialized knowledge but still have successful investment records because of their discipline and eye for value.

"Remember in May when James pointed out that to make money in the stock market you have to 'buy low, sell high'?" Roy asked us.

"It doesn't take a genius to figure that out," I replied.

"No? Then why do most market investors do the exact opposite? They buy high and sell low — a foolish approach if ever there was one."

"They lack self-discipline." Tom shrugged. "Stocks are low when almost nobody wants them. So to buy low, you have to buy at just the time when most people are saying it's not smart to do so."

"Exactly," Roy confirmed. "It may be the only law that has never been broken — the law of supply and demand. When a stock's price is low, it's down for only two reasons: there are too few buyers and too many potential sellers. In other words, the stock is relatively unwanted. To buy in that kind of environment takes a courage that few of us have."

"It's the same on the sell side," I broke in strongly. "You're supposed to sell high. When is a stock high? It's high when everyone wants it. It's high when demand is high and supply is low. It's not easy to sell a stock when all your co-workers and neighbours are telling you what a great buy it is."

"Can you see why discipline, which I define as the courage to buy when others are selling and to sell when others are buying, is so important? Without it, you're just another sheep . . . and you're probably heading toward a slaughter," Roy warned us.

" *Buy low, sell high* is impossible without self-discipline or 'courage,' as Roy calls it," James Murray summed up.

"How about *buy high, sell higher?*" Tom suggested.

"Certainly it's possible, but for obvious reasons, buying low is a much less risky proposition. Many people have lost small fortunes buying late in a market rally — buying high, that is — because they convinced themselves that 'this time it will be different.' That fateful phrase has cost a lot of people a lot of money. Attempting to buy high, sell higher, is simply a fool's game" was Roy's vigorously stated philosophy.

"I would be worried about *buy low, sell lower,*" I admitted. "I mean, after all, aren't most stocks low just before they drop off the board?"

"True, Dave," Roy responded supportively. "Just before a gas tank hits empty, it does pass through low. That's why, along with discipline, to be a prosperous investor you must also have that eye for value. You have to recognize the difference between an investment, say, a common stock, that's undervalued and one that just isn't healthy. There are many unwanted, hence low-priced, investments that are unwanted for good reason. For example, you could show courage by buying a home in Buffalo's Love Canal district, but I think you'll agree that that might also demonstrate a poor eye for value."

"What about real estate? There it seems that for the most part, buying low and buying value aren't that important. The operative expression seems to be, *buy at any price, sell higher."*

"Quite honestly, Tom, I can't put up a strong argument against your point. With the exception of some one-industry towns, real estate prices have been on a steady climb for fifty years. Sure, during tough economic times and recessions, values have suffered, but not much. In some areas, it seems that a bad year is defined as a twelve-month period during which home values rise only slightly. That being said, I'd like to add the following: most real estate investors have enjoyed solid returns throughout the past half-century, but the ones who have exercised discipline and bought value have been even more successful. Yeah, the guy who bought an overpriced duplex towards the end of an economic boom probably did sell it for a good profit several years later. However, the canny investor who located a bargain property and bought it during a recession will have reaped even greater rewards.

"Also, and I urge you to heed my words here, in my opinion the halcyon days of guaranteed easy money in real estate are coming to an end. As I mentioned in our conversation on home owner-ship, no trend is permanent. There's no law that says real estate can't decrease in value. I grant you that over the long term, well-selected real estate should always perform well. Note the term *well-se-lected.* If you use discipline and common sense and buy value, real estate will treat you well. But I don't think buying property without regard to location, timing, and value will continue to be a profitable strategy." Roy was quite adamant about this pre-diction.

"What worries me, Roy, is that I don't think I have the qualities you're talking about. I certainly don't have the knowledge, and I have no reason to believe

I have either investing courage or an eye for value . . . especially the latter."

"Don't worry, Dave," Roy reassured me. "As I said earlier, one of the prerequisites for a sound, productive financial plan is that its successful implementation not require tremendous investment management skills on the part of the plannee."

"I remember that point vividly." I grinned. "It gave me great comfort."

"Look at your financial plan and Cathy's," Roy continued. "You're both using professional money management, forced saving, dollar cost averaging, conservative RRSPs, a shortened amortization, proper insurance coverage . . . you know, all the boring things that make people wealthy. What in that plan calls for any complicated investment decisions? Before you answer, remember that your short-term savings for things like cars and trips are to be invested in guaranteed products."

"I see your point, Roy, but what if down the road Sue and I have a lump sum to invest . . . say, an inheritance or royalties from a travel guide that Sue might write?"

"And what about me?" Tom cut in. "Because I'm buying real estate with my ten percent fund, I'm forced to make investment decisions. I don't have the safety net of dollar cost averaging."

"That's right, Tom, you don't," Roy answered, seemingly ignoring the fact that I had posed a question before Tom. "I pointed out in May that when you elect to buy real estate with your ten percent fund, timing does become an issue. The discipline and eye for value we spoke of earlier are both important and, for reasons I just explained, will probably become even more so in years to come. That's the bad news. The good news is that you do seem to demonstrate those qualities. You've bought a property in an area that hadn't been subject to the recent run-up in prices, and what's more, you've bought a property that James described as one of the better values he had seen."

"I'm flattered that you feel that way, Roy. Unfortunately, my purchase had more to do with luck than wisdom. I didn't — "

"Yes, you did!" Roy stopped Tom abruptly. "You did recognize that property represented good value. I remember you saying that with the size of the lot, the proximity to the water, and the nice neighbourhood, the property was definitely underpriced. Don't you? James pointed out today that the eye for value is more often intuitive than informed. This is especially true of real estate investors. Quite a few people seem to have a knack for locating potentially profitable properties. Boy, how's that for alliteration?"

"Pretty powerful," Cathy quipped.

"Another intelligent thing you did, Tom," Roy continued, "was to consult James for an opinion. His success is a testimony to his ability to spot the _right_ property."

"Getting back to humble little me," I tried again, "what about my lowly question? I don't have Tom's eye for value, and even if I did, I probably wouldn't use it. I don't want to be an investor, I want to be a teacher."

"Yes, even though our plans are designed to diminish, if not eliminate, the necessity for investment skills, there could possibly be times when you are faced with an investment decision. Your example of an inheritance was a good one, Dave." Roy stopped speaking long enough to get the attention of Jimmy, who was half-asleep. "Jimmy, if someone finds him or herself with excess cash from an inheritance or from any other source, including savings from cash flow, what's the wisest investment he or she could make?"

"Pay off consumer debt," Jimmy shot back.

"No doubt about it," James Murray seconded.

"There is simply no better investment alternative for the average Canadian than to pay off his or her consumer debt . . . including the mortgage. The reasons are many. First and foremost, paying off consumer debt offers a great return on your money . . . not good, great! This is one of the simplest yet least understood concepts of proper money management. Interest on a consumer loan, be it a car loan or a mortgage on a noninvestment property, is not a tax-deductible expense. That means that the twelve percent interest you're paying to your bank for your furniture loan is being paid off with after-tax dollars. So if instead of paying off that same loan, you decided to buy a guaranteed investment certificate, what rate would the GIC have to pay just for that choice to result in a break-even proposition?"

Roy's question drew no immediate response.

"*Twenty* percent," Cathy finally blurted out. "If I bought a GIC paying twenty percent, because I'm in roughly a forty percent tax bracket, I would then earn twelve percent after tax. That's the same rate of return I am essentially *earning* by paying off my twelve percent furniture loan."

"Bravo! Do you two understand?"

Tom and I nodded.

'Something just struck me," Tom said thoughtfully. "If paying off a twelve percent consumer loan equates with earning a twenty percent interest return, just think what interest you would have to get to break even in paying off a credit card debt. Some of those cards are charging as much as eighteen percent on outstanding balances. You'd have to earn a *thirty* percent interest return just to come out even!"

"Now I ask you, is that complex mathematics? No, of course not," Roy answered his own question. "Yet incredible numbers of Canadians who have outstanding consumer loans also own Canada Savings Bonds and guaranteed investment certificates that pay fully taxable interest. It often doesn't make any sense. Mr. X buys $10,000 worth of CSBs that are paying six percent. After paying tax, he's lucky if he's keeping four percent. At the same time, he's paying his credit union loan off at thirteen percent interest with *after-tax* dollars. C'mon!" he scoffed.

"Knowledgeable investors agree that a three percent after-tax real rate of return is very good. Incidentally, what do I mean by *after-tax real rate of return*?" Roy quizzed.

"The absolute rate of interest less the amount paid in taxes, less the inflation rate," Tom expounded. "Basically, it's the amount you're gaining in purchasing power."

"Impressive. By paying off a twelve percent consumer loan, your after-tax rate of return is that same twelve percent, because the loan was being serviced with after-tax dollars. Let's say inflation is six percent. The after-tax real rate of return becomes, therefore, six percent . . . twice what is considered to be quite acceptable."

"I have a question. Should you always pay off the highest-interest-rate consumer loan first?"

"Dave, it should be common sense that if you have some money available to pay down consumer loans, you should pay down the one with the highest interest rate. Yet many people put $2,000 down on their eleven percent mortgage and leave their eighteen percent credit card balance untouched. Yikes! Yes, always pay off the loan with the highest associated interest rate," Roy answered diplomatically.

"There are a couple of other major considerations here," James Murray cut in. "Not only does paying down consumer debt offer an excellent rate of return, but it is also *guaranteed*, and there is a zero PITA factor. Reducing debt also reduces stress, and if that debt happens to be a mortgage, eliminating it also contributes to pride of ownership. It's a great feeling to own your home free and clear. The bottom line is that for most people, paying off consumer debt is the best investment alternative."

"Well, I'm glad that paying off consumer debt is a wise move because it's certainly the strategy that I feel most comfortable with . . . no heavy analyses, zero PITA factor . . . and, hey, eventually it'll free up my cash flow for other things."

"That's the benefit I've enjoyed the most," Jimmy reported. "Since I paid my mortgage off, I've increased my ten percent fund to a fifteen percent fund, and I still have a high disposable income. In my mind, the freed-up cash flow is the most satisfying benefit of paying off consumer debts."

"And to think we didn't even mention it, James," the wealthy barber remarked, chortling.

"What if we reach a point where we have money to invest and we have no consumer debt?" Cathy's red face betrayed the fact that she was somewhat embarrassed by her question. However, with her lucrative income, the hypothesis was valid.

"Jimmy?" Roy redirected the question.

"Years ago, I found myself in just that position. I had accumulated several thousand dollars and I had no debt . . . not even a mortgage. I went to Roy and asked him for some specific investment advice. You won't believe what he told me to do. 'Spend the money!' He told me to spend it! Now that's my type of financial planner," Jimmy concluded, giving Roy the thumbs-up sign.

"His fifteen percent fund was growing nicely, as was his RRSP. He had no debt. He had no need for life insurance. His daughter's education was secure. In short, all his financial goals were being met. I suggested that he go out and buy something he'd always wanted . . . a toupee perhaps."

Roy's advice to Jimmy didn't surprise me at all. In April, Roy had stressed that a well-designed financial plan should meet our future goals without dramatically lowering our current standard of living. In view of that, Roy's suggestion to spend it made perfect sense. Why shouldn't people live to the fullest once their financial futures are well taken care of?

"If you find yourself in the enviable position of having more money than you care to spend, I strongly recommend that, rather than investing it all at once, necessitating a correct investment decision, you spread out the investment by increasing your ten percent fund monthly savings. Let's say you had an extra $5,000. Put $200 more each month into your preauthorized chequing plan. Obviously, the $5,000 will eventually run out, and then you'll have to revert to your normal monthly saving amount. In the meantime, though, you will have invested your money wisely, taking advantage of the same strategies we've discussed before, and once again, you will have avoided having to time an investment purchase precisely."

It was hard for me to get excited about Roy's last bit of advice. Although I'm sure that I'm now on the road to financial prosperity, the point at which I will have more money than I care to spend is still years away.

Roy whisked me off as I stepped down from the barber chair. "On to income taxes?" I asked, anticipating his next topic.

"I have a question first," Tom interjected. "Don't we ever get to buy a penny stock or something that's fun like that?"

"Mark Twain once wrote, 'There are two times in a man's life when he should not speculate: when he can't afford it, and when he can.' If you want to play the market, buy commodities, or buy options on gold — don't do it under the guise of financial planning. Yes, it can be fun. Yes, it can be exciting, and yes, very occasionally it can be profitable. The same things can also be said of a trip to Las Vegas. And I should add, Las Vegas serves free drinks and is full of long-legged showgirls. Go to Vegas." Roy does have an effective way of driving a point home.

"Before we move on to income taxes, I want to share an idea that came to me the other day . . . an excellent idea," James Murray began modestly, as he set aside the real estate section of the paper. "As you know, the only piece of Roy's financial planning advice that I've chosen not to follow is his recommendation to place RRSP dollars in ownership investments. I still maintain that, from a diversification standpoint, it doesn't make sense to have all your long-term savings in one basket. My ten percent fund includes equity-oriented mutual funds. I own several properties and I invest most of my RRSP dollars in guaranteed vehicles. In my RRSP, I'm primarily a loaner. Because the interest earnings are allowed to compound tax-free until withdrawal, my RRSP has grown significantly. Cathy, you indicated that you, too, have decided to go the guaranteed route with your RRSP dollars. And though you two didn't say so, I sensed some apprehension on your part about having an entirely equity-based RRSP."

"With all due respect, Roy, I have to confess that James's diversification argument, combined with the manner in which RRSP deposits can compound tax-free, does make being a loaner look like an attractive alternative." I agreed with Tom, and was glad he had spoken up.

"I still favour ownership, but I'll repeat that if there is one place a loaner can prosper, it's in an RRSP . . . And the diversification argument has some validity,"

Roy admitted somewhat reluctantly. "What's your 'excellent idea,' James?"

"First, once your RRSP is worth $10,000, open a self-administered plan. Then buy a guaranteed investment certificate within the plan for the entire available amount — not just any GIC, but a monthly-interest GIC. Then open a monthly preauthorized chequing plan with a properly selected mutual fund for the same amount as the monthly GIC interest. Instead of all the money being automatically withdrawn from your bank each month, it will come from your self-administered plan. Each year, as you contribute to your RRSP and repeat the process, alter the PAC amount accordingly. It's beautiful — all your capital is guaranteed, yet you're still reaping the benefits of ownership, dollar cost averaging, professional money management . . . the works. It's tidy — there are no small amounts of money left sitting idly by. It's easy — twenty minutes of work a year, and no complicated investment decisions. Essentially, what you're doing is compounding your GIC interest into ownership. It's a great compromise!"

All eyes turned to Roy. "Hmm . . . That is one of the best ideas for investing an RRSP that I've heard." James Murray smiled broadly. "You're right, James, it is an excellent compromise for those people who want to be loaners in their RRSPs."

I had found my RRSP investment strategy.

"So the mutual fund shares would accumulate each month in your self-admin plan?"

"That's right. I'm not sure that all companies offering self-admins would be open to this idea — it is a lot of paperwork, but I'm sure something could be worked out with some of them. Sounds great, eh?" James Murray patted himself on the back.

"Certainly worth looking into . . . Now on to our favourite subject." Roy brought us all back to earth. "Income tax."

"A dollar saved is two dollars earned," Roy repeated his familiar refrain.

"That was last month's lesson, Roy. We're covering income tax now, remember?" Tom joshed.

"A dollar saved is two dollars earned, whether it's a dollar saved through coupons or through reduced tax," James Murray mused. "What's more, a tax dollar saved is one less dollar for the government to spend, not one less dollar for you to spend."

"What James means by that is that normally to save a dollar we must make some sacrifice, but when we save a tax dollar, there is no associated sacrifice. Tax savings are savings of the best kind," Roy clarified. "Because of that, it's important that each of you does your best to minimize your tax bill . . . your legal best, that is. Tax evasion is illegal and is not recommended. In fact, the almost epidemic proportions that tax evasion has reached through nonreporting of all sources of income is one of our country's major economic woes.

"On the other hand, tax avoidance, the minimizing of one's tax bill through the proper handling of one's financial affairs, is an important part of financial planning."

"I hate to keep playing the devil's advocate," I broke in somewhat sheepishly, "but I have even less interest in becoming a tax expert than I did in becoming a knowledgeable investor. The mere mention of the word *accounting* makes me shudder."

"Once again, your nervousness is unfounded," Roy assured me.

"We have said that one of the prerequisites of a sound and productive financial plan is that its successful implementation not be dependent on expert investment management by the plannee. Another prerequisite is that the successful implementation not be dependent on the plannee becoming a tax expert." Tom offered an almost perfect imitation of the wealthy barber.

"You must have studied financial planning under a brilliant mentor, Tom," Roy said with playful admiration. "What Tom just said is very true. Producing and following a sound financial plan should not be dependent on the plannee being a tax expert, not just because becoming a tax authority is an arduous task, but also because for most of us there are very few *tax tricks* that are worth knowing. No matter how knowledgeable about the tax system we may be, we have very few opportunities to legitimately reduce our tax burden."

"Even chartered accountants pay standard amounts of personal income tax," James Murray pointed out.

"Unless you run your own business, I can teach you a lot of what you need to know about income tax in a matter of minutes."

"I do run my own business, and so does Sue now. What about us?" Cathy pleaded.

"The tips I'm going to give these two should still be of some help to you, but there is one other tip you should take very seriously — see an accountant!" Roy instructed forcefully.

"I have an accountant," Cathy told him, adding, "an excellent accountant . . . a handsome accountant. He does all my personal and business returns, calculates how much I should draw out of the business each year, creates quarterly balance sheets and income statements, keeps me informed . . . and looks great."

"It's *imperative* that a business owner work closely with a qualified accountant. A good accountant is worth his or her weight in gold . . . and most are good. The professionalism and training in the accounting field are unparalleled. Accountants are not selling products, they're selling expertise, so their advice tends to be unbiased. If you're a business owner or someone whose financial affairs are very complex from a tax standpoint, enlist the services of an expert! I can't stress that enough."

"I think you just did, Roy," Tom noted.

"Tom, you'll look great in a mohawk," Roy threatened. "What can you two boys do to reduce your taxes?"

"RRSPs," I answered. "An RRSP contribution reduces taxable income, and a spousal RRSP can be a really effective way of reducing income taxes."

"Very good, Dave. Tom?"

"Take advantage of the $100,000 capital-gains tax exemption by saving ten percent of all you make and investing it for growth in equity funds."

"Aside from making RRSP contributions and taking advantage of the $100,000 capital-gains tax exemption, there are only two worthwhile ways that I know of for the average Canadian to legally reduce his or her tax bill."

"What do you mean by 'worthwhile'?" I wondered.

"Well, there are some ways to reduce your taxes that are perfectly legitimate, but often not worth the time or effort. An example — tax experts are always recommending that you defer the receipt of income to the next tax year, whenever possible. They reason, correctly, that by deferring your tax liability, you are keeping the use of your money for an additional year. If Tom's brother earned $1,000 on the side in December doing some trimming, it would be wise for him to request payment in January. By deferring the tax liability for one year, Brian would have twelve months to use the $400 he would have had to pay in taxes. Four hundred dollars could earn forty dollars interest . . . less sixteen dollars in tax . . . twenty-four dollars. Hey, twenty-four dollars is twenty-four dollars, but the average person is not going to spend a lot of time tax-planning for that type of money.

"I'm certainly not saying this type of planning is a waste of time — I do it. Remember, 'a dollar saved is two dollars earned.' However, for most people, this may be taking tax-planning a bit too far."

"I agree, Roy, but what if someone could defer the receipt of $10,000?"

"Obviously, that's a much different case, Cathy. The average Canadian, though, doesn't have the opportunity to defer anything close to that amount of income." Very true. Most of us are wage earners who are happy to accept pay cheques whenever they're offered.

"So what are the two worthwhile ways?" Tom probed.

"The first is proper income-splitting. You don't have to be a math professor to understand that as much income as possible should be claimed by the lower wage earners in the family."

"Hey, Roy," I blurted out, "you're not going to believe this, but I know a fair amount about that stuff!"

"You're right; I don't believe it." Roy chuckled.

"A friend of mine taught me the basics of income-splitting last year. Because I earn more money than Sue, all our savings accounts are in her name. That way, the taxable income those accounts earn is taxable in Sue's hands, not mine."

"Your example of income-splitting is well taken. Over the years, that type of planning can save people significant sums of money."

"What can Cathy and I do, income-splitting-wise?" Tom tossed in. "We don't have spouses or children to split with."

"Get married."

"Get married to avoid income taxes . . . Roy, you're such a romantic." Cathy shook her head. "Then again, I wonder if my accountant would be game?"

"If you and Tom married each other" — Roy was showing his bias — "you could pay him a small salary for doing your books, thereby reducing your taxable income."

"Yeah, but I'd be increasing Tom's taxable income by the same amount," Cathy argued.

"True," Roy granted, "but it's the same concept as in Dave's savings account example. Tom's taxable income would be increasing by the same amount as yours would be decreasing, but because you would be in a higher marginal tax bracket than Tom, it would result in significant tax savings.

"Proper income-splitting is just a matter of using your head. It's just common sense. If Sue's earnings are lower than Dave's, then of course we want the savings accounts in her name."

"I don't think my father understands income-splitting," Cathy said, jumping in. "All my parents' savings are in Dad's name, and he's in a much higher tax bracket than Mom. I'm going to tell him to switch that around immediately!"

"Whoa, now!" cautioned Roy. "That's a waste of time. It contravenes the *attribution rules.*"

"Attribution rules?" Cathy echoed. "What are those?"

"If income-producing property is transferred by a low-interest loan or by gift from one spouse to another or to anyone under eighteen years of age, the recipient's income from that property is taxed in the hands of the donor. In addition, if an income-producing property is transferred via a low-interest loan to a *nonarm's-length* party — a relative, regardless of their age, the income is again taxed in the hands of the donor. The attribution rule also applies to capital gains in a spouse-to-spouse transfer," Roy explained.

"That's unfair!" my disappointed sister groaned.

"Not really, Cathy," Roy responded. "In fact, the

attribution laws are very fair. It's through your dad's earnings that those savings were created, so they should be in his name — and taxed in his name."

"What about Dave and Sue? You said it was a good idea for them to keep their savings accounts in Sue's name. Don't the attribution laws apply there, too? I mean, Dave is making more money than Sue. Wouldn't those savings more likely be his? Or shouldn't at least a hefty percentage be in his name?"

"Thanks, Sis. I appreciate all you're trying to do for me . . . or should I say to me?"

"There is some logic in what you're saying, Cathy, but no, the attribution rules wouldn't apply in Dave's case. You see, Dave could easily argue that the money in the savings accounts was saved exclusively from Sue's income and that his income was used to pay the bills. Whereas, in your parents' case, with your mom never having worked outside the home, that argument wouldn't wash."

"What if Mr. Richardson lied?" Tom suggested. Roy just sighed.

"As I said a minute ago, the attribution rules are fair. Without them, each family could arrange their affairs in such a way that the government would be able to collect very little tax on investments and savings."

"Sounds good to me, Roy," Tom tossed in.

"It doesn't sound so good to the sick, the needy, the unemployed . . . all those who require government assistance. And it wouldn't be fair to future genera-tions, who will already be saddled with a huge debt."

"You do believe in paying your fair share of taxes, don't you, Roy?" Tom surmised.

"I certainly do, Tom — *fair share* being the key term. I have nothing against organizing your finan-cial affairs in the wisest possible way to minimize your tax liability; however, tax evasion is a whole different ball game. It's illegal and irresponsible. What's more, it's unnecessary if you do proper financial planning."

"As Roy said earlier, proper income-splitting just comes down to using your head," James Murray reiterated. "I pay my wife a salary for keeping my books and doing all my secretarial work. It's perfectly legitimate — she really does work for me — and it's a very effective tax strategy. Out of my hands and into hers, so to speak. Another example: several years ago, I had $10,000 sitting in my savings account from a commercial real estate deal. My daughter was fifteen, so I gave her the money to buy a three-year compounding guaranteed investment certificate. Why? Because when the GIC matured she would be eighteen, so the attribution rules wouldn't apply. The interest earned was taxable in her hands, not mine. As a university student, she had a low taxable income and ended up paying *no* tax on the interest gain. I would have paid handsomely! It was only logical to plan that way."

"I should point out a few things about James's last example," Roy added. "One: it is no longer available as interest must now be claimed every year. Two: the government lost out on this manoeuvre, but so did James. If he had invested the money in his own name, he would have had to pay tax; however, even after tax, he would have made some return. By giving the money to his daughter and letting her spend the income, he avoided tax but he also missed out on earning a return for himself. Essentially, he helped his daughter out and got the government to partially subsidize his generosity. Three: had he given his daughter the money and then asked for the repayment of the principal and the investment gain, he would have been breaking the rules — it would have been a low-interest loan. Four: if you implement a strategy for the sole purpose of avoiding tax

the government may deem it inappropriate and reverse it. In James's case, he gave Karen the money
not only to avoid taxes, but also to help her through
school, so everything's fine. Five: if you give someone
money, he or she is under no legal obligation to give
it back. Never forget that! That $10,000 is now
Karen's.

"Now let's move on to the second way the average
Canadian can reduce his or her tax bill — become
knowledgeable about all the deductions and credits
available to you! Before you start harping at me
about not wanting to become accountants, let me
add that to become knowledgeable in this area takes
only a few hours of reading, not a few years of
schooling. Just read your government-produced tax
guide, and consider buying and reading one of the
many available tax tips books. There are several of
these easy-to-read books that list dozens, or even
hundreds, of oft-forgotten potential deductions.
James, for instance, didn't realize that he could
claim tuition expenses for some of the correspon-
dence courses he was taking, until he carefully read
his tax guide. The tax savings amounted to hundreds
of dollars."

"Doing the reading Roy is recommending may take
five hours, but I'll guarantee you that you'll find at
least one deduction that you haven't been taking
advantage of. Your gains per hour of reading will be
quite rewarding. And remember what a dollar saved
is," James Murray reminded us.

"A final point about tax planning — "

"I thought the section on tax planning was supposed to be as long as the section on investing," Tom
chided Roy with a grin.

"You three didn't ask as many annoying questions
during the section on tax planning. Besides, Tom,
you're thinning up top," Roy shot back, also with a
smile. "Now I'd like to briefly discuss tax shelters.

Technically defined, a tax shelter is any investment that enables investors to claim a deduction, loss, or tax credit that may be applied to offset income from other sources. The tax deductions, credits, or incentives won't usually cover the entire cost of the investment. So if the investment proves to be a poor one, economic loss may result."

"Have you ever thought about writing a textbook, Roy?" Cathy teased.

"I realize that definition was somewhat technical, but it was also very accurate. I gave that definition to you so it would be clear to you that a tax shelter is nothing more than an investment. Yes, there are certainly tax implications, but all those tax considerations serve to do is to reduce your investment cost — your out-of-pocket cost. If the investment performs poorly, you could still be a loser despite the associated tax relief. Losing a dollar to save fifty cents is not an intelligent move.

"Why do tax shelters offer tax relief? Because, for the most part, if they didn't, nobody would buy them. The tax breaks serve as an incentive to buy — a needed incentive. That is to say that by their very nature, tax shelters tend to be risky propositions. In addition to having a higher level of risk than most other investments, tax shelters are usually complex. Not only do you have to understand the tax implications, but you also have to understand the investment merits and you have to do battle with our old foe — timing."

"Are you saying not to ever buy a tax shelter, Roy?"

"No, I'm not saying that, but I am saying this: before you ever buy a tax shelter, make sure you have seen a professional!"

"An investment expert or a psychiatrist?" I quipped.

"Both," Roy answered half-seriously. "And for heaven's sake, don't buy a tax shelter until the rest of your financial house is in order . . . no mortgage, a substantial RRSP, a growing ten percent fund, et cetera.

"I don't want to sound harsh here, but it's hard not to. For every success story in tax-shelter invest-ing, there arc nine horror stories. It's darn hard to figure out which tax shelters are going to be profit-able! The prospectuses for tax shelters often read like the space shuttle owner's manual." Roy glanced at James Murray for support.

"Don't buy tax shelters!" James concurred with conviction. "I don't normally like to give blanket advice, but in this case, it's warranted. Sure, by following my advice you'll occasionally miss out on a good investment — but you'll also miss out on dozens of bad ones. Believe me, I know!"

This particular advice was wasted on me. I have now, and had then, no intention of ever buying a tax shelter. I'd buy a bomb shelter first.

"So what's on the agenda for our last month, Roy?" Cathy wondcred. "Miscellaneous topics?"

"Yes, there are three or four topics you still need a bit of information about. Then, of course, Clyde will present each of you with a hand-engraved, solid-gold plaque denoting your graduate status from the Miller School of Financial Planning. The plaque can either be wall mounted or it can stand on a table — "

"Opportunistic pupils probably melt it down and sell it at the bank," interrupted the ever-enterprising Tom.

"I may have taught that lesson on thrift too well," Roy muttered, shaking his head.

|10|
GRADUATION

"Oh, you shouldn't have," Clyde protested modestly. "I really didn't do all that much."

"Something tells me that that beautifully wrapped package isn't for you, Clyde," speculated James Murray. "It's for me."

"Nice try, guys," I replied. "This token of our appreciation is for Roy, in recognition of all that he has done for us. Admittedly you two, and even Jimmy here, have also been big helps to us in our quest for financial independence. For all you've done for us, we'd like to present you with our heartfelt thanks. We were going to buy each of you a gift, but as has been pointed out so often, 'A dollar saved is two dollars earned.' "

"Igor, ve 'ave created a monster!" James Murray spoofed.

"You three really didn't have to buy me a gift." Roy blushed. "My reward is seeing you on the road to financial prosperity."

"That's exactly what I said, Roy, but Dave and Cathy wouldn't listen," Tom reported, straight-faced.

"Yeah, yeah . . . Dave, my boy, climb up into the chair and let's get started. There are four miscellaneous topics I want to touch on and then, of course, there's my world-renowned wrap-up speech."

"But James already delivered that rhetoric a couple of months ago, Roy. Can't we just skip your version?" Tom kidded.

"No" was Roy's concise response. "Now, it really doesn't matter which of the four topics we start with — "

"Back when we covered life insurance, you promised we would take a look at disability insurance this month," Cathy politely reminded Roy. "Let's talk about that first."

"Sure, Cathy," Roy agreed, to indulge her. "Disability insurance is the most neglected of all forms of insurance, yet for many people, it's the most critical insurance need. What are your chances of being disabled for a one-year period at some point in your life?"

"One in twenty?" Cathy guessed.

"I would say one in thirty," Tom speculated.

"One in four," Roy stated solemnly, taking the three of us aback.

Cathy broke our stunned silence. "That's amazing."

"It really is," Roy concurred. "A thirty-year-old has a one-in-four chance of becoming disabled for one year or more at some point in his or her life.

"At your age, your biggest asset by far is your earning power. You have to protect it. If a machine in your basement churned out 40,000 one-dollar bills a year, would you insure it against breakdown? Of course you would, especially if you knew there was a twenty-five percent chance that it would quit on you. Are you with me?"

We nodded vigorously.

"When people die, they cease to be a financial asset to their dependants. That's why so many people need life insurance — to replace that asset — to replace that earning power. When people are disabled, they

don't just cease to be an asset to their families —
they become a liability. Excuse me for being blunt,
but dead people don't need to be fed, clothed, or
sheltered. Nor do they demand the constant medical
care required by many disabled people. Make sure
that you have proper disability insurance coverage!"

"I'm covered through work," I announced. "You
probably are too, Tom."

"Be careful about that assumption, Dave," Roy
cautioned. "Many employer group plans offer insuf-
ficient coverage. In addition, they are often nonport-
able. If you left your place of work to go out on your
own or to go to an employer who did not provide
adequate group disability coverage, you would have
to hope that you were in good enough health to
qualify for an individual disability policy."

"How can I tell whether my group plan is adequate?"

"It isn't easy. Disability insurance policies are
complex. However, there are some basic questions
that you should seek answers to. If you receive a yes
to all of them, your policy would seem to be a good
one. For example, is the loss of hearing, sight, speech
or of the use of two limbs considered to be total
disability under your group policy? Is disability defined in broad terms? Is the policy noncancellable?
Is there a waiver-of-premium clause? If so, does it
extend beyond the benefit period? Is the only policy
exclusion an accident of war? Does the policy provide
benefits during rehabilitation? Are the benefits indexed?"

"Slow down, Roy! Where do we find out about all
this?" Tom took the words right out of my mouth.

"Talk to your personnel department. They should
know the answers to most of those questions, and if
they don't, they'll know where to find them. Also,
show your group policy to an insurance agent who
can help you compare its pros and cons with those
of an individual policy."

"What if our group policies are inadequate?" Tom pressed on.

"If your group policy is inadequate, Tom, or if you are not even a member of one, you will have to buy an individual policy. Most life insurance agents are well versed in the area of disability insurance. Moreover, there are agents who specialize in designing disability insurance programs. Either source should be able to advise you on the plan and options best suited to your needs."

"How much coverage should we have?" I queried.

"Because benefits from disability policies purchased by individuals are tax-free and because, for obvious reasons, insurance companies like to maintain a gap — an incentive, if you will — between what you were making before being disabled and what they'll pay you while you are disabled, you're generally restricted to insuring between sixty and seventy percent of your gross income, less any benefits already in force."

"Is that a run-on sentence?" I asked in my most formidable teacher tone.

"What about car, fire, and content insurance? Any advice in those areas?"

"Of course, Cathy. See your general insurance agent," Roy instructed her with a friendly wink.

"Miscellaneous topic number two: saving for your children's education," Roy said, moving on. "Saving for your children's education is a relatively straightforward process — "

"It sure is, Roy," Tom interrupted. "Don't do anything and let the kids earn their way through school."

"How callous!"

"Not really, Cathy," I defended Tom. "There are all kinds of people, Mom and Dad among them, unfortunately, who believe that children should pay their own way through postsecondary school. I paid my own way, and though I wasn't too thrilled with our parents' stance at the time, I realize now that it was good for me. I learned the value of hard work and discipline. Today I'm proud to say that I put myself through university."

"What a martyr," Cathy snorted. "The only reason Mom and Dad didn't help you out was that they thought you were going to flunk out."

If I hadn't suspected that to be the case, I would have offered a scathing comeback.

"Regardless of the parents' motives, as Dave said, there are all kinds of people who place on the child the responsibility of paying for a postsecondary education. In fact, I'm one of those people. However, I will admit that, for a variety of reasons it isn't always possible for the student to shoulder the whole burden. A postsecondary education is expensive and even a hard-working, independent student can't always raise the needed funds. So though I feel it's primarily the student's responsibility to put him or herself through school, I also feel that any parents worth their salt would help out, if necessary. Fortunately, putting yourself in the position of being able to help out is a very easy and very inexpensive part of financial planning.

"One of the most effective ways to save for a child's education is also one of the simplest. Place a small amount of money, as little as twent-five or fifty dollars a month, in your name, in trust for a child with a well-selected equity mutual fund."

"Forced saving, good long-term growth potential, dollar cost averaging, the capital-gains exemption — it's all there," I broke in.

"Exactly, Dave," Roy confirmed. "The key variable when deciding whether to go the equity fund route is on your side — time. You've got a fifteen-year investing period. By the way, why do I say fifteen years instead of eighteen?"

"I know," Tom declared. "Murphy's Law again! For

the same reasons we don't want our RRSP dollars in equity funds just prior to needing the money, we don't want our education fund in equity funds just prior to our child going on to a postsecondary school. If the market were to take a dive, we wouldn't have the luxury of being patient; we'd be forced to rush out when the market was low. It's better to redeem the needed funds several years in advance, at a time when you see the market is strong — sell high, you know."

"So once our child is fourteen or fifteen, we should watch for an opportune time to redeem, do so, and then roll the funds over into guaranteed investment certificates," I summarized.

"What about the attribution rules?" Cathy asked.

"They don't cause much of a problem because, as I pointed out last month, the attribution rules don't apply to capital gains earned by a child. Admittedly, the mutual-fund holding does generate a small amount of dividend and interest income each year. However, it's a relatively insignificant amount," Roy responded patiently.

"What do you think of Registered Education Savings Plans, Roy? Are they worthwhile?" My question elicited strange looks from Cathy and Tom, who must never have heard of RESPs.

"RESPs," Roy explained to my two baffled companions, "are registered plans to which you contribute after-tax dollars, meaning that you receive no tax deduction. However, with them, as with RRSPs, the government does allow investment earnings to accumulate tax-free while in the RESP. When your child enters a qualified postsecondary institution, an amount based on your total plan value is paid from the RESP to the child for each of the three or four years. That paid-out amount is then taxed in the child's hands."

"That's great!" I enthused. "Another way to income-split legitimately!"

"True," Roy said hesitantly, "but in my opinion, not always the wisest way. By using the method I've just described, you can not only save for a child's education, but you can also save tax dollars — without exposing yourself to the risk that's inherent in an RRSP."

"What risk? I thought RESPs were normally invested conservatively," I argued.

"What if your child doesn't pursue a postsecondary education? Then you'll receive only your RESP contributions back, and you will *not* get the earnings on them for the period your money has been in the plan. That kind of income-splitting, where it's your *income* that splits, is not recommended. Mind you, many financial companies are now offering very flexible RESPs that allow any number of beneficiaries per plan, and the beneficiaries can be changed at any time. Those same plans also often have very diverse investment alternatives. But while there's no denying that RESPs are a much-improved product, I'm still not totally sold on them."

"I decided against an RESP for my daughter because at the time I wasn't sure that she would go on to college or university. I analyzed the situation and reasoned that for me at least, buying an RESP was too risky. I didn't want to lose the potential investment earnings."

I could see James Murray's point. Having a father who is a high school principal makes you acutely aware of the fact that less than fifty percent of the population goes on to postsecondary education. However, because RESPs have become so flexible, I'm still going to look into them.

"All right, onward we go. Miscellaneous topic number three: emergency funds — "

"I was wondering when you would get around to that topic," Cathy said excitedly. "Don't they always say that the average person should have a readily available emergency fund equivalent to three or four months' gross income?"

"Ah, the mysterious 'they' again." Roy sighed. "Many financial planners do recommend building and maintaining an emergency fund of that size, Cathy. Why? I don't know. To me, it makes little sense to have upward of $10,000 sitting around earning fully taxable, low rates of interest. You would be much better off to use those funds to eliminate consumer debt or to fund your RRSP. Really, with the exception of a job loss or, for the business owner, an extended *down period*, what emergency could possibly call for $10,000?"

"What if the wind blows the roof off your house one night?"

"You're covered by insurance."

"What if your car breaks down and needs repairs?"

"Ten thousand dollars worth?"

"What if your furnace dies on the coldest night of the year?"

"Get it fixed" was Roy's uncomplicated advice. "It sure won't cost you ten grand. Look, I'm not against emergency funds, but I do feel that $2,000 to $3,000 is much more realistic than $10,000. If you're afraid that an expensive emergency looms in your future, establish a $10,000 line of credit at your bank. That way, if you really do end up needing the money, and I doubt that you will, it will be there for you. In the meantime, you're free to invest your funds in more productive ways.

"Having said that, let me repeat that it is important to keep a few thousand at your fingertips. Minor emergencies not only can happen, they do happen! Especially if you're a homeowner! Also, if you have a couple of thousand in the bank and you see some item on special that you really want, you can buy it. People with small bank balances are too often forced to pass up excellent bargains. And finally, having a couple of thousand in the bank is good for your peace of mind. People sleep less soundly at night knowing that they have only $168 in their account."

"What do you mean, 'only'?" Tom added, chuckling.

"Roy, you mentioned that a business owner would be wise to have a substantial emergency fund. Does that include me?" inquired Cathy.

"Obviously any business owner or commissioned salesperson whose income is unpredictable, varying widely over time, is smart to 'save for a rainy day.' It's surprising the number of stockbrokers, for example, who during good times raise their standard of living to match their temporarily high income level and don't set aside any funds to help carry them through the inevitable bad times. Cathy, whether or not your business is cyclical in nature is your call.

"People who have little job security are also smart to maintain a substantial emergency fund. Again though, that decision rests with the individual involved."

"Another thing worth keeping in mind here, Roy " — James Murray took over — "is human nature. All too often it subverts the purpose of an emergency fund. The temptation to convert the emergency fund to a travel or boat fund is just too strong for most of us. The old needs-versus-wants conflict again."

I could certainly see that happening!

"Miscellaneous topic number four: staying informed." Roy moved on efficiently. "Yes, your financial plans are very straight-forward in terms of both implementation and maintenance. But it certainly can't hurt to keep abreast of the major goings-on in the world of finance. Certain events could occur that might dictate a change in your planning philosophy. For example, the person managing your mutual fund could die. You might then want to reevaluate your choice.

"As I said months ago, there are several excellent sources of financial information available in Canada, including the *Financial Times*, the *Financial Post* and the daily business section of the *Globe and Mail.* These publications aren't just informative: but they're also entertaining. The world of finance is dynamic, colourful, and fascinating!"

"Roy, can't you just do all the reading and keep us informed about anything pertaining to our financial futures?" Tom's idea sounded pretty good to me, but judging from the look of mock dismay on Roy's face, it didn't to him.

"All right, Clyde, drum roll, please. After seven long months, this is it. We've come to the end of the Miller course in financial planning. And much to my delight, you've all passed with flying colours. However, before Clyde presents you with your diplomas, I'd like to make a closing remark . . . or two." Roy paused to step out from behind the barber chair.

"Over the past seven months I've taught you the basics of developing a productive financial plan. The strategies that I've outlined for you will serve well any Canadian between the ages of twenty and forty-five. They will do so regardless of occupation, regardless of income level, regardless of previous financial knowledge, even regardless of mathematical, investment, and accounting skills.

"This comprehensive plan's strength lies in its simplicity. Anyone can understand and apply the principles that we've discussed. And unlike most financial plans, ours goes beyond the mathematics of saving and investing to take into account human nature. Its success is not dependent on unrealistic expectations having to be met by the plannee, the way so many others are. I recognize that most people don't like to budget and that they don't enjoy constantly monitoring investments. I accept that most people enjoy blowing some money from time to time.

I also understand that most people feel a great deal of stress when they're burdened with a high level of debt.

"The very simplicity of the plan troubles some people. 'How can anything so readily understood work so successfully?' It works because it's born of common sense. This plan allows us to move toward the attainment of all our financial goals by taking advantage of unglamorous but highly productive concepts.

"Dave, when you first approached me, you said that you wanted to achieve the average Canadian's goals of a nice home, a prosperous retirement, an education for your children, and at some point you wanted to enjoy the finer things in life. You wanted to accomplish this without having to be a financial genius, and without a substantial reduction in your current standard of living. Do you feel that you have learned how?"

"Mission accomplished," I acknowledged appreciatively.

"The bottom line is simply this," Roy concluded. "Fancy tax shelters, straddle-option strategies and future contracts on gold all make for great conversation at cocktail parties. Forced saving, dollar cost averaging, and compound interest simply make for great cocktail parties."

Roy's "bottom line," as he called it, was greeted with a standing ovation.

"Encore! Encore!" Tom shouted. "Teach us a family planning course now!"

"First, you'll have to find a wife, Tom. Now please be seated," Roy protested. "Clyde, the certificates, please."

"You were serious about diplomas?" I asked, startled. "Wow, this is great! Hey, Tom, your first diploma!"

"Ha, ha!" Spending so much time at the barber

shop had still not made Tom's comebacks razor sharp.

Clyde proceeded to hand to each of us a beautifully framed, official-looking diploma from the Miller School of Financial Planning. He shook our hands and commended us for having taken the top three spots in our graduating class. Despite Clyde's kidding, the three of us were elated with our performances.

"As I'm sure you've noticed, we have a little something for you, too, Roy," I announced. Cathy presented Roy with a nicely wrapped package that obviously contained a framed picture.

Roy opened it deliberately, so as not to tear the gift wrapping.

"Going to reuse that paper at Christmas?" James Murray joked. "The virtue of thrift, and all that stuff."

When the picture was finally visible to him, Roy's eyes became misty. My talented sister had painted the front view of Roy's impressive house, capturing it in the warm glow of a Lake Huron sunset. The engraved gold plate adorning the frame read simply, "The Rewards of Common Sense."

"This is wonderful . . . I'm deeply touched . . . I just love it . . . My wife will want it hung in the main living room, for sure. You shouldn't have," an emotional Roy insisted.

"It was the least we could do for our financial mentor," I said sincerely. "We owe a great deal to you."

"In fact, we owe our good fortune," Tom said with a smile, "to *the wealthy barber!*"